St. Augustine and the Civil War

St. Augustine and the Civil War

Robert Redd

The History Press

Published by The History Press
Charleston, SC 29403
www.historypress.net

Front cover, bottom: Courtesy Library of Congress.

First published 2014

Manufactured in the United States

ISBN 978.1.60949.897.9

Library of Congress CIP data applied for.

Notice: The information in this book is true and complete to the best of our knowledge. It is offered without guarantee on the part of the author or The History Press. The author and The History Press disclaim all liability in connection with the use of this book.

Contents

Acknowledgements

St. Augustine, Florida, is a city with nearly 450 years of history. The city has changed hands multiple times, each time adding to the historical legacy of the small coastal town. There are strong cultural roots that show everywhere ranging from African Americans to Minorcans. Many aspects of St. Augustine history have been written about and already well documented, with further research taking place every day. However, with a city as old as this, there are always opportunities for further investigation.

When I first came upon the subject of St. Augustine and the Civil War, I didn't really know what, if anything, happened there. My knowledge of Florida Civil War history taught me that no major engagement happened there. To leave it at that didn't seem right, however, so I poked around a bit and found that really very little had been written. I thought there had to be stories of interest; a town as rich and proud of its history as St. Augustine must have something to say.

And does it! From army generals, to seemingly racist religious leaders, to first ladies and former presidents, to shipwrecks, to women willing to speak their minds, it was here. It became a matter of tracking it all down and putting pen to paper, so to speak. What I feel I have accomplished is really just scratching the surface. There is more there, and further research can pull it out. Hopefully, this brief volume can spark the interest of others in this seemingly ignored period of St. Augustine history, and they can delve deeper into individual topics.

I, of course, couldn't have done this alone, and there are many people to thank. For anybody wanting to pursue research in St. Augustine history, you must visit the St. Augustine Historical Society Research Library. Here I was aided multiple times by Chief Librarian Bob Nawrocki, Senior Research Librarian Charles Tingley and Assistant Librarian Deborah Willis. During my first visit, they set me at ease, listened and asked questions, expressed interest and even suggested a better place for me to park on future visits. They are a wealth of knowledge, and if they don't know something, they express a real interest in learning about it. Also in St. Augustine is the Flagler College library. From there, I received tremendous help from Christine Wysocki, who provided a wealth of information and photos on property now owned by the college. Mike Stock at Trinity Episcopal Church shared what he knew about Edmund Kirby Smith's early years.

Locally, I am indebted to the ladies at the Edgewater Public Library, who helped obtain copies of several books through interlibrary loan. Learning how to do that was new to a couple of them, but every time I came back for a new book or to return one, they asked about my progress and if the book had helped. At the New Smyrna Museum of History, Executive Director Leigh Finner has been encouraging since we met, and Joan and Dave in the museum library have turned up items of interest that I would not have found without them. Thanks, guys, and I'll see you at the next meeting!

The help I have received from other libraries and repositories has been amazing. Everybody has been willing to help and provide copies and answers in a timely manner. In Florida, the ladies of the Martha Reid Chapter of the United Daughters of the Confederacy helped answer several questions. At the State Library and Archives of Florida, Tyler McLean and Miriam Spalding helped get me copies of large amounts of materials. Those unknown by name to me helped by providing Confederate Pension Records and digital copies of photos. James Cusick from the University of Florida provided copies of several documents and gave some advice on where to check for other items.

Early on, I met with success gathering information with the help of Victoria Ambrose at the New Canaan Historical Society, Nancy Mason at the University of New Hampshire, Lisa Nugent and Sierra Dixon at the Connecticut Historical Society, Diana Bachman at the Bentley Historical Library located at the University of Michigan and Jennifer Coleman at the Pearce Museum at Navarra College.

My last frenzied push for photographs was met with quick help from Frank Arre at the Naval Historical Foundation, who, despite the problems with the sequestration, was able to get my requested photos. Michelle Lambing from the Texas State Preservation Board provided multiple scans of little-known individuals in almost no time. The good folks at the U.S. Army Heritage & Education Center also had a very quick turnaround time, again on lesser-known individuals who I felt it was important to include.

To anybody I may have forgotten, it is unintentional, and I do appreciate the help you have provided. Despite the efforts of these wonderful people, any errors included would be my responsibility.

I have received encouragement from many friends and family. When I first announced the book project, I received encouragement from so many friends, both personal and those I have made online, that I can hardly begin to thank them all. Please know, however, that I appreciate the kind words from all of you.

I must, however, give special thanks to my friend Jim Schmidt. Jim is the one who really pushed me to pursue a book-length project. He stomached his way through a couple ideas that really weren't right, some that just wouldn't have worked and at least one that was really beyond my first-time author's grasp. He guided me through the proposal process and critiqued what I had done. He never sent back a negative word yet got his points across about where I could improve my plan before submitting it. Lo and behold, I got the green light! Thanks, Jim, I owe you one if you ever make it to Florida or I make it to Texas.

To Chad Rhoad and everybody else I have dealt with or will deal with at The History Press, I thank you. You have been supportive of a new guy, and I appreciate it. I hope this book repays the chance you have taken on me.

My parents, Theodore W. and Bonnie G. Redd, have been supportive the whole way. Thanks for instilling in me the work ethic you have and the fortitude to stick this out. Your words "Do good work" ring in my ears!

Last, but certainly not least, my thanks and love go to my beautiful wife, Christina. Civil War history isn't her interest, yet she has always listened to me when I made what, to me, was an interesting find. She was also a willing trooper during many cemetery trips in St. Johns County, even when the days started getting longer and hotter. She was often the one who would find a headstone and was a tremendous help as we created a GPS database of Confederate burials. Her ideas helped clarify the walking tour included in the book. Overall, the book would not be what it is without her input, and for that I am grateful!

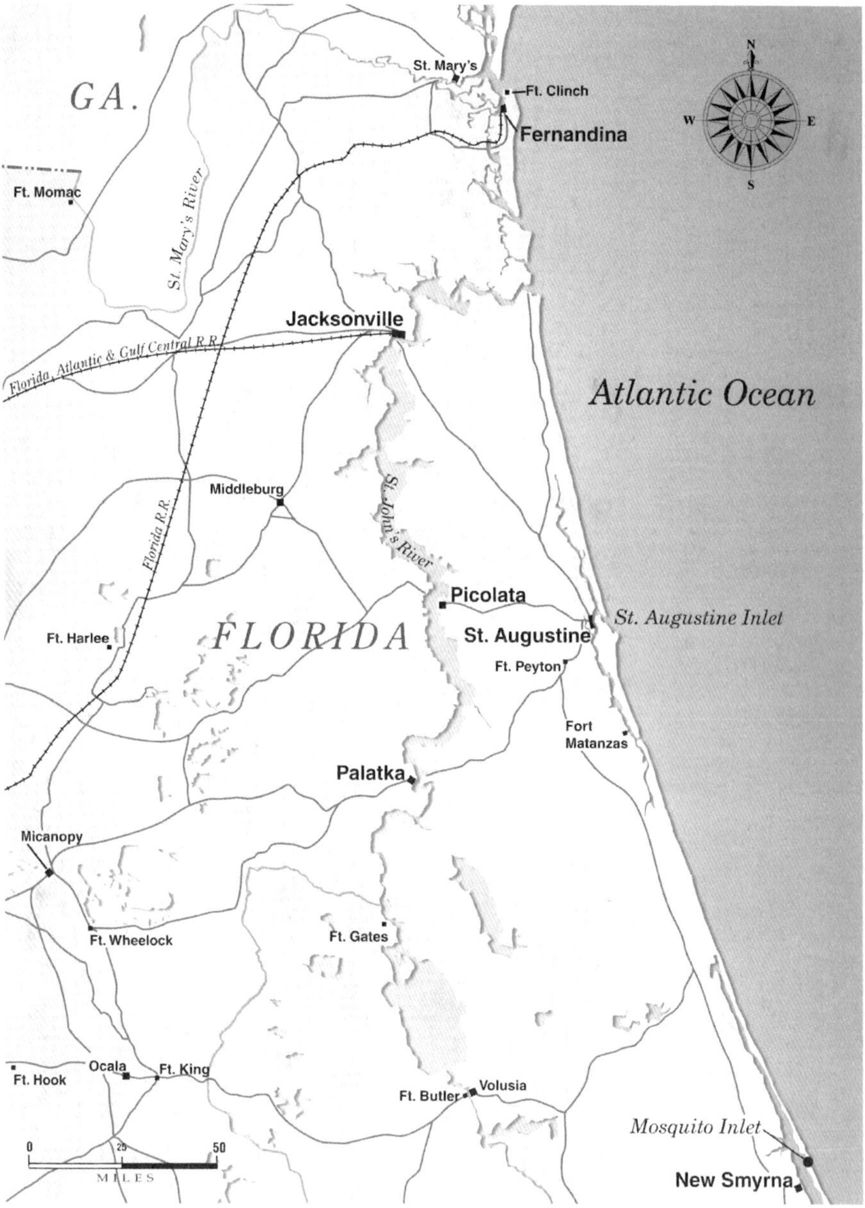

Map of eastern central Florida by Steven Stanley.

Chapter 1

STATEHOOD AND SECESSION

Southern men and Southern women will not sit down with folded hands if the masses elect a Black Republican President," predicted St. Augustine resident Frances Kirby Smith, mother of future Confederate general Edmund Kirby Smith, in early 1860.[1] Little could she have known how true her words would soon be. By the end of the Civil War, more than 650,000 men would be dead, including 44 hailing from her adopted town of St. Augustine, Florida.[2]

Despite its long history, Florida had only joined the Union in 1845 as the twenty-seventh state. Florida was lightly populated and by 1850 had approximately eighty-seven thousand people, both free and enslaved. This small population was smaller than many northern cities such as Chicago, Philadelphia, New York City and even Baltimore. Despite being new to the Union and having little in the way of capital and manpower, the state was ardently behind the secession movement and was quick to take action.

In Florida, like other states, numerous events led to a secession convention: the Compromise of 1850; the actions of abolitionists, in particular John Brown and his raid on Harpers Ferry; and, most importantly, the election of a "black republican" president in Abraham Lincoln. Quickly on the heels of South Carolina calling for a convention, Florida governor Madison Starke Perry requested the Florida legislature to act quickly and do the same. It agreed and set December 22 as the date for delegate elections. The men elected were to be in Tallahassee on January 3, 1861, to make a crucial decision for the state.[3]

Drawn portrait of Madison Starke Perry, the fourth governor of Florida. He served from October 1857 to October 1861 and called the Florida Secession Convention. He later served as colonel of the Seventh Florida Infantry. *Courtesy State Archives of Florida.*

The only loud opposition came from former Florida governor Richard Keith Call. He called secession "treason against our Constitutional government." By signing the Ordinance of Secession, he claimed that these men had "opened the gates of Hell, from which shall flow the curses of the damned to sink you to perdition." He was a firm Unionist and claimed, "I pray that in the hour of death, the Stars and Stripes may still wave over me, and wave forever over our whole united country."[1]

The men elected from St. Johns County were Rhydon G. Mays and Matthew Solana. Mays was a fifty-eight-year-old planter born in South Carolina. According to the 1860 United States Federal Census, he had real estate holdings of $20,000 and personal property worth $100,000. According to the slave census for the same year, an R.G. Mays in Putnam County was the owner of eighty-eight slaves. Putnam County is adjacent to St. Johns County, so it is most likely that these are the same

Former Florida territorial governor Richard Keith Call was an outspoken opponent of secession. *Courtesy State Archives of Florida.*

man. The 1860 census lists Matthew Solana as owning $4,000 in real estate, with a personal estate valued at $20,600. He was the owner of thirty slaves. These statistics would clearly point to which way St. Johns County would cast its votes. The men were backed up by the *St. Augustine Examiner*, which proclaimed, "What shall Florida do? Secede of course!"[5]

The body of sixty-nine men chosen to attend the secession convention, while seemingly diverse, was for the most part heterogeneous. All were, of course, white men. The average age was 42.5 years. Only seven delegates were Florida natives. Georgia and South Carolina were the most heavily represented, claiming thirty-six delegates. Thirty-two members were classified as farmers or planters, seven were lawyers, ten were merchants and four were physicians. The median value of real and personal property combined was $22,000, so the St. Johns County delegates would have been considered wealthier than the average delegate. Fifty-one members of the convention were slaveholders.[6]

The questions facing secession conventions across the South were not would a state secede but rather how and when would it. The options facing the men in Tallahassee were whether to secede immediately or to delay and seek cooperation with other states. In Florida, it has been estimated that approximately 60 percent of the delegates were considered immediate secessionists.

Fire-eater Edmund Ruffin was an avowed secessionist who believed strongly in slavery and states' rights. As the end of the war neared, he killed himself rather than live under "Yankee rule." *Courtesy Library of Congress.*

While the majority of conventioneers arrived on January 3, 1860, as appointed, fifteen had not. Because of this and the next day being a day of fast, it was voted to adjourn until January 5. On the appointed day, the elected men met and were joined by the "fire-eater" Edmund Ruffin from Virginia and, later, South Carolina. Ruffin was an ardent supporter of states' rights and a proponent of secession. He attended the hanging of John Brown and is sometimes credited with firing the first shot at Fort Sumter. On January 5, Ruffin's birthday, he was given a seat in the convention hall despite making a weak protest against such.[7]

The first order of business was to elect a president, and this was done by a vote of 59–10 in favor of secession supporter John C. McGhee from Madison County. Rules of procedure were then adopted, and E.C. Bullock from Alabama and L.W. Spratt from South Carolina were welcomed. These men were representatives of their states sent to Florida to observe the convention.

When the convention met again on Monday, January 7, McQueen McIntosh, a former federal judge from Calhoun County, submitted a resolution declaring the right and need for secession. This passed by a margin of 62–5 after attempts by the cooperationist wing to wait for action by Georgia and Alabama were denied. A thirteen-man committee was appointed to draft an ordinance of secession. Also on January 7, both Bullock and Spratt gave speeches in favor of secession, and then John Pelot, a conventioneer from Alachua County, put forth a motion that Edmund Ruffin address the gathering. Ruffin, who later claimed to not be prepared

The Southern states were in a huge rush to be near the first to secede or, in the case of this editorial cartoon, jump over the edge from the Union. Some were not as sure, as shown by the rider wanting to take a different route. Original print by Currier & Ives, 1861. *Courtesy Library of Congress.*

to give a speech, spoke on the importance of Florida and other lower South states acting quickly on secession in order to convince upper South states such as Virginia to secede as well.

On January 9, the thirteen-man committee presented its report and called for the immediate secession of Florida from the Union. The cooperationists then attempted to attach amendments. George Ward, from Leon County, moved that the ordinance should not take effect until after committees in Georgia and Alabama met. A.K. Allison then submitted that if Georgia and Alabama did not secede, Florida voters themselves would have to approve the ordinance. Both motions were voted down, as were several other feeble attempts to delay the inevitable.

The Florida ordinance of secession was passed on January 10 by a margin of 62–7. It was then that Jackson Morton of Santa Rosa County, J.P. Anderson of Jackson County and J.W. Owens of Marion County were elected delegates to the Montgomery Convention in order to help form the Confederate government. The convention then adjourned until February 26, when it reconvened to consider the ratification of the Confederate constitution. The constitution was approved unanimously, 54–0.[8]

In becoming the third state to secede, after South Carolina and Mississippi, Florida had now cast its lot and for many years would bear the consequences of this decision.

Chapter 2

The War Years

The citizens of St. Augustine quickly heard the news that Florida had seceded from the Union as the *Examiner* announced on January 19, 1861: "It is done. On Saturday afternoon several of our citizens who arrived from Tallahassee where the State convention had assembled and is now in session, brought us the intelligence that the Secession Ordinance had been passed by that body, declaring that Florida withdraws herself from the Confederacy of states existing under the name of the United States of America."

The majority of citizens of the town were pro-secession, and they certainly had a strong backer in Matthias Andreu, publisher of the local *Examiner* newspaper. The motto of the paper before secession was "Equality in the Union and Nothing Less." By late 1860, Andreu was putting forth that the South had no choice but to withdraw from the Union due to aggressive abolitionists bent on freeing the slaves. In November, he had gone so far as to suggest that "the day is possibly not distant, when such talk will be punished as treason, and it is not improbable, some one of them may adorn a gallows."[9]

This period of time was one of both great hope but also great nervousness for citizens. With the announcement of secession and the subsequent bombing of Fort Sumter, the citizens of St. Augustine felt the right to be proud of their young "country," and a new flagpole was erected in the Plaza. Mrs. Cooper Gibbs supervised the making of a new flag to fly here. The Catholic Church, led by pro-slavery Bishop Augustin Verot, believed that a religious revival was taking place in the city. Men were joining militia groups boasting of being willing to fight the Yankees. Things were looking up for the Confederacy in the eyes of those in St. Augustine. Neither the men nor the proud women supporting them could have predicted what was to come.

The first action in St. Augustine was in many ways a non-event but again served to boost Confederate morale. With the Secession Convention winding down in Tallahassee, Governor Madison Starke Perry sent orders for Fort Marion to be taken. On January 7, 1861, Ordnance Sergeant Henry Douglas penned a letter to Colonel H.K. Craig outlining what transpired:

> *I am obliged to perform what is to me a painful duty, viz, to report to the Chief of Ordnance that all the military stores at this place were seized this morning by the order of the governor of the State of Florida. A company of volunteer soldiers marched to the barracks and took possession of me, and demanded peaceable possession of the keys to the fort and magazine. I demanded them to show me their authority. An aide-de-camp of the governor showed me his letter of instructions authorizing him to seize the property, and directing him to use what force might be necessary.*
>
> *Upon reflection I decided that the only alternative for me was to deliver the keys, under protest, and demand a receipt for the property. One thing certain, with the exception of the guns composing the armament of the water battery, the property seized is of no great value. The gentleman acting under the governor's instructions has promised to receipt to me for the stores.*[10]

The first great takeover of the fort was accomplished by the Rebels without a single shot being fired. The next day, many of the invaders returned to Fort Clinch at Fernandina, taking with them several of the large guns used to protect Fort Marion.

Despite the outward signs of bravado, there was an undercurrent of uneasiness as well. While true that the majority of citizens supported the cause, there was need to be on the alert for those continuing to be loyal to the Union. A "vigilance committee" was formed whose goal was to watch for slave agitators and others speaking against secession. Those who supported the Union, such as the wealthy Clarissa Anderson, thought it best to keep their thoughts to themselves and protest silently by means such as unsubscribing from the newspaper. Northern visitors, whom the city depended on for economic survival, were looked on with caution and sometimes scorn, as shown by Mrs. Frances Kirby Smith: "These abolition scamps do not hesitate to enjoy our fine climate & hospitalities (when they can get them) hating us inwardly, and outwardly doing all they dare."[11]

As 1861 wore on, the economic reality began to hit home as well. In March, newly inaugurated President Abraham Lincoln's plan to regain any Federal property seized by the Confederacy sent concern through the city, as did the newly instituted naval blockade. For most of the war, St. Augustine was patrolled by ships belonging to the South Atlantic Blockading Squadron led by Samuel F. DuPont and later by John A. Dahlgren.

Samuel DuPont led the South Atlantic Blockading Squadron at the start of the war. His success led to his promotion to rear admiral in 1862. *Courtesy Library of Congress.*

Blockade running became a profitable, albeit dangerous, career option for many men. Blockade runners were used in many different ways. They might be transporting goods such as cotton to countries that would pay much-needed cash. Blockade runners might have also been used to transport needed goods such as salt, meats,

John A. Dahlgren served as chief of the Bureau of Ordnance and, later, commander of the South Atlantic Blockading Squadron. He is most famous for the cast-iron muzzleloading cannon that bears his name, like the one he is shown standing with. *Courtesy Library of Congress.*

The *Teaser*, shown here at Fort Monroe, Virginia, is an excellent example of what a blockade runner would have looked like. *Courtesy Library of Congress.*

vegetables and firearms to other parts of the Confederacy. Many runners were also bringing needed items such as food and medicine. They may also have been loaded with luxury goods that the South did not have the ability to produce.

Blockade runners typically differed in appearance from standard transport ships. They were usually longer but overall smaller and had shallow drafts. This would allow them to be more maneuverable and quicker than the ships pursuing them. They would also be able to disappear into shallow bodies of water such as creeks and inlets.

The majority of blockade running was done at night. This prompted the Confederate government to order all lighthouses to be extinguished, despite the fact that the lights helped the runners navigate the sometimes dangerous coast line. It was reasoned that the lights were a bigger help to blockaders trying to prevent the runners from entering or exiting harbors.

Lighthouse keepers have always been loyal to their duties to protect the men at sea, and many of the keepers ignored the order to extinguish their lamps. Locals, however, became quick to take this order into their own hands when keepers would not act. Paul Arnau, the customhouse officer in St. Augustine, organized a group that became known as the "Coast Guard" and set about to dim the lights along the east coast of Florida.[12]

Paul Arnau resigned as mayor of St. Augustine in the days before the Union arrival. He later was responsible for dimming the lights in many East Coast lighthouses. He is buried in Evergreen Cemetery in St. Augustine. *Courtesy the author.*

The group started locally at the St. Augustine Lighthouse. The keeper at the time was Maria de los Delores Mestre Andreu. She had become the keeper in 1860 after her husband, Joseph, plummeted to his death while whitewashing the outside of the light tower. Her appointment to the keeper position was met with approval from the local newspaper: "We are sure that this appointment will commend itself to all as a fast and kind recognition of the services of her much respected deceased husband and as a just provision for the support of a poor and deserving widow who has been deprived of her stay and support."[13]

Her time as keeper was brief, however, as the Arnau group removed the lenses from the tower and hid them. The "Coast Guard" worked its way south, next stopping at Cape Canaveral, where it forced keeper Mills O. Burnham to dismantle the various lenses. Burnham, however, did not destroy any of the mechanism, instead crating the pieces and storing them on his property. The men continued south, reaching Jupiter Inlet, where the light was still operational. Keeper Jose Papy, a Unionist, refused to cooperate and would not even dim the light. The Arnau gang gathered support from

The original St. Augustine lighthouse was completed in 1824. By 1870, erosion was threatening the tower, and the current tower was erected and operational by 1874. The original tower was washed away in 1880. *Courtesy State Archives of Florida.*

local resident James Paine, along with assistant keepers Oswald A. Lang and Francis A. Ivy. The large, and now armed, group convinced Papy to leave his post and then dismantled the light, hiding the pieces. The group still had one more target: the Key Biscayne lighthouse. This light was dismantled, and the men returned to their homes. Arnau reported their deeds to Florida governor Madison Starke Perry before returning to St. Augustine, where he served as mayor from 1861 until early 1862, before the Union occupation.[11]

While blockade runners did occasionally make it through, cities like St. Augustine were affected almost immediately. The city was dependent on food imports from the North that were now forbidden. Locals, who already grew much of their own food, were forced to plant even more in hopes of feeding their neighbors. Food prices soared due to scarcity and a lack of currency. Citizens wrote letters to friends in other areas of the state in hopes that there would be goods available to be sent. A public subscription was taken up in order to help the poor afford even the most basic of food items. By 1863, an out-of-town reporter observed, "The harbor is deserted, save when an occasional Government transport makes the echoes with its shrill steam whistle, or a little fishing shallop comes or goes."[15]

Another casualty due to the hostilities was the tourist trade. The winter of 1861–62 saw a tremendous drop in the number of Northern visitors. These visitors would have brought much-needed capital to the city. Instead, the hotels and businesses remained empty. The *Examiner* suggested that the city market itself as a summer resort for Southerners rather than an area for Northerners to escape the frigid winter.

An 1861 letter seems to sum up the situation in St. Augustine shortly after secession:

> *These "secession" movements have made quite a revolution in & about this "ancient City." Once it was the resort of many invalids & strangers, but is now wholly deserted by them. Those who reside here are in very straightened circumstances & live "from hand to mouth." Provisions are very scarce & dear & those who are not too poor to move seem determined to leave. Without giving further details I can only say that "St. Augustine" is far from a desirable place to live in.*[16]

The fate of St. Augustine, and truly Florida in general, was sealed by Robert E. Lee in late 1861 when he decided that only the ports of Brunswick, Savannah and Charleston were worthy of being defended. In February 1862, many Florida troops were ordered north, and in March 1862, Lee declared, "The small force posted at Saint Augustine serves only as an invitation to attack." Despite all the negativity from the Confederate government and the poor economic climate, the majority of people in St. Augustine remained loyal to the cause.[17]

On February 28, 1862, a fleet of twenty-six U.S. Navy ships left from Hilton Head, South Carolina, with the goal of occupying coastal towns in southern Georgia and northern Florida. On March 8, the steamer *Keystone*

The men from the *Penguin* (in the far left of the photo) along with the *Henry Andrew* were involved in a skirmish at New Smyrna that led to the death of five Union sailors. When Union ships returned in 1863, the city was shelled, destroying almost everything there. Originally published in *The Soldier in Our Civil War*, vol. 1, page 189. *Courtesy U.S. Naval Historical Center.*

State, under the command of W.E. LeRoy, arrived off the sandbar. The next day, LeRoy sent a smaller craft to search for passage through the tricky area. Not finding a way through the difficult-to-navigate waters, the boat returned to the main ship.

This short break allowed the Third Florida Company B Infantry, also known as the St. Augustine Blues, time to leave the area. They marched south to the small city of New Smyrna just south of Mosquito Inlet. While in New Smyrna, they helped protect a shipment of arms and also fought in a minor engagement that killed several Union men. This skirmish was remembered in 1863 as Union ships took aim at the Sheldon Hotel located atop a small shell mound near the waterway. No citizens were killed in the 1863 revenge shelling, but it did remind those in lands controlled by Confederates that they were never safe.[18]

On March 11, 1862, Commander C.R.P. Rogers and men from the USS *Wabash* braved the ocean and sandbar, rowing a longboat into town flying a white banner of truce. They were met by a white flag flying from the pole at Fort Marion. When Rogers and his men arrived at the wharf, they were met by acting mayor Christobal Bravo, who had been named mayor just a week earlier after the resignation of loyal Confederate Paul Arnau.[19]

Christobal Bravo was born around 1807 in Florida and at the time of the war worked as a merchant. In later life, he worked as a farmer. His son, Christobal M. Bravo, served as a corporal in the St. Augustine Blues until he was discharged for having heart disease upon surgeon's certificate of disability in July 1862. The younger Bravo would pass away in 1871 at the age of twenty-nine. He is buried in Tolomato Cemetery in St. Augustine.[20]

Above: The USS *Wabash* delivered Union troops to St. Augustine in March 1862 to demand the surrender of the city. Commander C.R.P. Rogers was met by a flag of truce, and no shots were fired as the Union took control of the city. *Courtesy Library of Congress.*

Right: Acting mayor Christobal Bravo helped oversee a smooth surrender of the city to Union forces. His son, Christobal M. Bravo, served in the Third Florida Company B, "St. Augustine Blues." The younger Bravo is buried in Tolomato Cemetery. *Courtesy the author.*

Mayor Bravo greeted the unarmed Union soldiers and escorted them to the Government House, where the city council had gathered to hear the surrender terms. The terms were rather simple in that they could continue to govern their town as long as they accepted the law and authority of the United States. These terms were quickly agreed to, and at the suggestion of Commander Rogers, a United States flag was raised over Fort Marion, signifying the city was now under Union control.

This quick turnover of the city to Union forces did not sit well with one of St. Augustine's oldest and most revered women, Frances Kirby Smith: "'Old Bravo' the mayor, she reported in disgust, and the council, 'much like him, all low ignorant Minorcans, puffed up by their devotion to office, had raised the white flag as soon as two row boats rounded the point—and afterwards assisted in raising on the Fort their flag.'"[21]

For the second time in two years, the city of St. Augustine had peacefully changed hands. While the surrender may have been peaceful in that no shots were fired, that does not mean that all were happy. Many of the women of St. Augustine were particularly upset. As Rogers was surveying the town, many voiced their displeasure with the Yankees, yelling and spitting at them. The secession flagpole, so proudly raised just the prior year, was chopped down so that the flag of the United States would not be raised upon it. While Rogers took this in stride, he did report to his superiors his overall thoughts on the political views of the citizens:

> *I believe that there are many citizens who are earnestly attached to the Union, a large number who are silently opposed to it, and a still larger number who care very little about the matter. I think that nearly all the men acquiesce in the condition of affairs we are now establishing.*
>
> *There is much violent and pestilent feeling among the women. They seem to mistake treason for courage, and have a theatrical desire to figure as heroines.*
>
> *Their minds have doubtless been filled with the falsehoods so industriously circulated in regard to the lust and hatred of our troops.*
>
> *On the night before our arrival a party of women assembled in front of the barracks and cut down the flagstaff, in order that it might not be used to support the old flag.*
>
> *The men seem anxious to conciliate us in every way.*[22]

With the Union now firmly in control of St. Augustine, the first in a series of Union regiments arrived in the city. The arrival of the Fourth New Hampshire, under the command of Colonel Louis Bell, signified a huge shift in power in the city. Union supporters were now free to speak their minds, while those still supporting the Rebels had to watch themselves. As stated by Confederate supporter Hannah Jenckes, "These times will work wonders, make some of us discreet and stayers at home."[23] One of the first to encounter the wrath of Union forces was lighthouse dismantler and former mayor Paul Arnau, who was imprisoned until he returned the lighthouse lenses.

Louis Bell was born in 1837 and came from a highly respected New Hampshire family. His father was Governor Sam Bell, and siblings included Dr. Luther Bell, New Hampshire senator James Bell and Chief Justice of New Hampshire Samuel Bell. Louis was an 1855 graduate of Brown University and in 1857 passed the bar exam and opened a law practice. At the beginning of the war, Bell enlisted and served as captain of the First New Hampshire Infantry Company A. In August 1861, he was appointed lieutenant colonel of the Fourth New Hampshire. He was next appointed inspector general and chief of staff by General Thomas Sherman. In March 1862, he was promoted to colonel.[24]

Brigadier General Thomas Sherman briefly served as Union commander of the South before being sent to the western theater of the war, where he served at Corinth, New Orleans and Port Hudson. After the war, he received the rank of brevet major general. *Courtesy Library of Congress.*

With the stationing of Union troops, some areas of life began to return to a sense of normalcy for the residents of St. Augustine. United States currency again became the accepted form of money for most businesses. Even at this early stage, Confederate currency was buying less by the day, with many merchants in town unwilling to accept it at all. Colonel Bell requested a supply of currency in order to help jump-start the local economy. At the request of locals, a post office was put into operation as well.

Despite the hope for a peaceful stay, Colonel Bell could not be sure to which government the citizens would profess loyalty. At the start, he felt it imperative that he show the might of the Union army. In a letter to his wife, he outlines the steps he took:

> *And at night I rest in peace with the key on my table and sentinals walking always along the walls, which within one hundred yards of the castle, is a town, (as near as from Mothers to Jo Websters) where at least three out of four of the inhabitants would be glad to see us all killed, and would be glad to attempt it, were it not for the loaded cannon that would destroy them in a moment, that look over the walls. Twenty four hours ago if an officer walked through this town, he was greeted with insulting remarks from every knot of citizens. Now, when I have notified the Mayor that all the guns were loaded, and trained on the city, ready to lay it in ruins in case of any disorder, and have arrested two of the most distinguished citizens for mere words against the Government, the streets are deserted in the evening, and not one man dares breathe one word against the Government.*

Bell himself was under no illusion as to what a lot of locals thought of him personally:

> *Since I have been here I have put the Fort in complete order, and the great black cannon say to the City, "we only wait for the word, to destroy you." Can you believe my own darling wife that the poor little boy who has held you to his heart, and who had always from childhood loved you, is looked on, by the citizens of St. Augustine as an ogre who must be obeyed from terror, and who would have no more hesitation in burying the women and children under the smoking and shot crumbled ruins of their houses, than in taking a walk.*

How much of his writing was truth and how much was McClellanesque bravado is hard to speculate. There can be no doubt, however, that in the early days of Union occupation there was certainly fear among the residents.

Bell did not think all in St. Augustine was bad, however, as he told his wife:

> *Yet St. Augustine is a most beautiful place, and the scenery—the oranges—lemons—dates and Bananas are a source of continual wonder to me, and the gorgeous tropical plants and the beautiful flowers I have not tired of, and though I never go out of my Fort without a guard to protect me, yet I constantly see curious things and strange customs that are a ceaseless source of interest to me, and would be to you were you with that husband who loves you so much.*[25]

Colonel Louis Bell, Fourth New Hampshire Infantry, kept firm control of the city of St. Augustine during his time there. Bell would later perish during the capture of Fort Fisher in January 1865. *Courtesy Military Order of the Loyal Legion—Massachusetts Commandery (MOLLUS-MASS) Photograph Collection, United States Army Military History Institute.*

It was under Colonel Bell that the oath of allegiance began to be offered to citizens. Bell, however, was not one to take the oath lightly, and he told one citizen, "If you take the oath of allegiance and afterwards prove false, if I can take you I shall shoot you as I would a mad dog, without a trial." Many times the oath would be taken more out of necessity rather than true allegiance, as was stated later by a historian of the Seventh New Hampshire: "Nearly all of the inhabitants who remained were dependent at once upon the Federal commissary for rations, and they were not backward in making applications for relief to a government they pretended to despise: but they were obliged to take the oath of allegiance to the United States before their wants were supplied." Reverend L.R. Staudenmeyer was vocal in his opposition to the use of the oath as a means of acquiring food: "Many families held out, to nearly starvation, and when the petty tyrant saw that many would not take the oath & would rather live on anything rather than even outwardly avow their fidelity to the Lincoln government the rein was daily more tightened. Merchants were not allowed to sell except to those that took the oath. The merchants were forced to take the oath to do business."[26]

The Union soldiers quickly made themselves at home despite the isolation from their Northern homes. Some of the soldiers wrote home or in diaries with glowing descriptions of the city. Elias Bryant, a musician from Francestown, described the weather and bountiful food that was available:

> *Our stay at St. Augustine was the pleasantest part of our army experience. We enjoyed the climate, which was like our summer, but in the warmest days the heat was tempered by the refreshing sea-breeze. I do not remember ever suffering with the heat as at the North, although, of course, the thermometer*

would stand much higher. As a rule, at four or five o'clock, we would have a severe thunder shower, with heavy reports and very sharp lightning.

We could supply ourselves easily from the hucksters or sometimes from the plantations themselves with oranges, lemons, figs, watermelons, muskmelons, pomegranates, and guavas. About every house in town had a large grape arbor. These would be covered with great clusters of purple fruit, which we could buy for what seemed to us a trifle. Oranges (sweet) were nearly done when we arrived but we had a taste of them at the plantations themselves. The sour oranges succeeded them and we soon cultivated a taste for these. They were made by the inhabitants into pies, which we found delicious. Mulberries grew on large trees, which were used sometimes as shade trees about the houses. These berries resemble blackberries. They were not offered for sale, not being very plentiful, but several times I was invited to help myself from the trees.[27]

Private Leander Harris, from Hampstead, had similar thoughts on the area in a letter home:

Tell father that people are hoeing here now, some of the corn is as high as my head. We have salad any time that we want it. Most all if not all kinds of tropical fruits, grow here, oranges, lemons, figs, pomegranites, dates, bananas and many other kinds, if we stay here till the season for them we shall live high. The weather is very warm, but there is a cool breeze every day which makes it quite comfortable. The warmest part of the day is from about 10 a.m. to 2 or 3 p.m. I generally take "siesta" then if the others will keep still enough.[28]

Harris's views on the city had apparently softened after a few days being in the city because a few days prior he had written to his wife:

You probably know that this is the oldest town in America, I do not recollect the date of the settlement, but to judge from the appearance of the place, should think it was about the year 1 B.C. There is nothing American in the looks of the town, everything appears just as it left the hands of the old Spanish settlers. There is an old convent with a Catholic Church close by, which has a chime of 4 bells, or rather what is called a chime, but a jangle would be more appropriate I think, for such an infernal clatter I have never heard before, as they made this morning calling the people to church. It sounded like a dozen cows, with each a cow bell on her neck, and going upon the run.[29]

The Cathedral Basilica of St. Augustine. Much of the church was gutted by fire on April 12, 1887. The church was rebuilt with the help of architect James Renwick. Original photograph by Samuel A. Cooley. *Courtesy Library of Congress.*

Despite the stated abundance of fruits and vegetables, the men wrote home about how the food situation was not pleasant for everybody, and even troops were concerned when stores got low: "The citizens, some of them, must be actually suffering for food as the Quarter Master was obliged to stop supplying them with any some days ago, indeed I do not know how long it will be before we shall be in the same situation ourselves, for we have but a few days rations left, But I feel confident there will be a boat in very soon."

With the blockade in place and Southern merchants unable to purchase Northern goods, stores ran low on items such as clothing. The same soldier, who must have been quite the dandy, wrote home with a request:

> *I should like to have you as soon as you receive this, send me 4 shirts, (you can buy one pair if you have not got them made) and a few good collars, some pocket handkerchiefs, two or three neckties, a half dozen prs cotton stocking a half dozen prs good shoes, congress boots, or some other good style, I can fit myself with one or two prs, and sell the rest at a good profit, I want a good pr black, or dark blue pants, Size waist 34 length 36, (if they do not fit I can have them altered.) and a good felt fur hat, low crowned and wide rim, Size 7⅜…I should like a good blue frock coat, but don't know how you would fit me. If I had the cloth I could get it made. I should like a pair of calf-skin boot, if you have not disposed of those that I sent home you may send them. If you have plenty of money handy you may buy a pair. If I do not want them I can sell them for a good price. I want a half ream of good writing paper, (about this size) and some envelopes, it costs too much to buy them here. I should like to have you put in some black and white linen thread and two or three spools of cotton, and a few skeins of black silk. There is nothing of the kind to be had here. Cotton has been selling for 25 cents a spool.*[30]

In addition to the regular marching and serving on picket duty, the men had to find amusements for a good part of their time in the town. Many played cards, read books and papers, wrote letters home to friends and loved ones or played in the regimental band; one soldier bragged that he had never heard a better band. The Fourth of July holiday was celebrated by the soldiers "in a very appropriate Manner. A grand procession was formed at 7 a.m. in which members from each Company took part in and marched through the principal streets and made a fine display. In the Eve had fireworks but of a poor quality."[31] The parade was led by the Knockemhigherthanakite Band.

Not all pastimes went well for the Fourth New Hampshire, however. A popular activity was swimming or boating in the river. During the early days of June, nine soldiers took a boat sailing in the bay area, and it capsized. Only six of the men were able to make it to safety, with three drowning. The men who perished, all from Company D, were Corporal Charles Chase Cofran of Northfield, Private Luther L. Libby of Gilmanton and Private John Lamay of Groton. According to diarist Private Henry Haskell, a soldier by the name of D. Stiles (possibly George D. Stiles of the Fourth New

Hampshire Company D) was found guilty of not paying attention to orders and was fined five dollars.[32]

As time passed, the residents of St. Augustine grew more accustomed to Union soldiers now living among them. That did not, however, mean that they were welcomed or that the locals backed them and their government. When local Episcopal reverend L.R. Staudenmeyer, who generally sided with the Confederate cause, was leaned upon to offer a prayer for Abraham Lincoln and the Union cause, he essentially sealed his removal from the city. Leading churchgoers, such as Frances Kirby Smith, refused to participate in services where prayers were said for "Old Abe." Fearing the backlash of locals, the Union troops suggested to Staudenmeyer that he leave the city. While he did not leave willingly at first, he did finally make his way north to Davidson College in North Carolina.[33]

As the summer ended, St. Augustine was to see a new group of troops arrive. The Seventh New Hampshire, under the command of Haldimand S. Putnam, arrived in September 1862.

ORDER OF EXERCISES
FOR THE CELEBRATION OF THE
86th ANNIVERSARY
OF
AMERICAN INDEPENDENCE
AT ST. AUGUSTINE, FLA.,
BY
The Fourth Regiment N. H. Volunteers.
JULY 4TH, 1862.

The Procession will be headed by the
Celebrated Knockemhigherthanakite Band!
under the direction of HERR SAWMYNOSEOFF, and will perform
GRAND POTPIEOWRONE
on the Plaza, on which occasion they will produce some of their most soulstirring and heartrending Melodies.

THERE WILL BE A DRESS PARADE OF THE
"HIGHLANDBLOWFISTICATORS,"
upon the Common in front of the Fort, at 6 o'clock, A. M., after which the "Highlandblowfisticators" will march through the principal streets of the City. They will then "bring up" at the Plaza, where an
ORATION
Will be delivered by PROFESSOR TWISTEMSTRAIGHTER.
After which DR. SAWBONES will present a MAGNIFICENT CROWNOMETER to the most intellectual-looking soldier in the ranks. Presentation Speech by P. BOWERS, President of the C. Y. L. O. Society.

AT 8 O'CLOCK, A. M.,
The Games of CATCHING THE GREASED PIG, CLIMBING THE GREASED POLE, WHEELBARROW RACE (Blindfolded), SACK RACE, and POTATO RACE, will come off as soon as the grounds in the rear of the Fort can be cleared of the "*Mushrooms*"

The Evening will be enlivened by a
GRAND DISPLAY OF FIREWORKS
on the Green near the Fort.

July 4, 1862, saw the Fourth New Hampshire Infantry celebrate the Independence Day holiday in St. Augustine with performances by the Knockemhigherthanakite Band, a speech by Professor Twistemstraighter and fireworks. *Courtesy University of New Hampshire Special Collections.*

Putnam was born on October 6, 1836, in Cornish City, New Hampshire. At age sixteen, he was appointed to the Academy at West Point and graduated with high honors, later serving on the western frontier. At the beginning of the war, he was commissioned a colonel in the Seventh New Hampshire Infantry. He would not survive the war, being shot through the head while leading a charge at Fort Wagner in July 1863.[34]

It was during early September that tensions escalated. A loyal St. Augustine shoemaker named Mr. Murray "was shot by the Gurrillars while milking his cow. Pickets fired on the gurrillars, did not get them."[35] This incident forced the Union hand, and all white males ages fourteen and up were gathered in the Presbyterian church. They were given the option to take and sign the oath of allegiance or be forcibly banished from the town. Several days later, a few hundred people, mostly women and children, were gathered together, having been declared disloyal. They were boarded on the *Burnside* and sent toward Jacksonville. They arrived at Jacksonville only to be returned to St. Augustine under the authority of General Alfred H. Terry. Terry ordered Putnam not to arrest sympathizers. Despite returning to the town, many

Union brigadier general Alfred H. Terry, commander of the Morris Island Division of the Tenth Corps. He helped raise two regiments of troops and fought at First Bull Run, Petersburg, New Market Heights and other battles. *Courtesy Library of Congress.*

saw the writing on the wall and left under their own free will. No effort was made to stop them.

This new, more lenient policy toward Confederate sympathizers lasted for only a few months before Putnam was again forced to crack down on enemies of the Union. The new order called for all families with men in Confederate service and those with known pro-Confederate feelings to be prepared to leave in one week's time. Those forced to leave were let off at stops including Fernandina, St. Mary's, Brunswick, Beaufort and Hilton Head.[36]

The men serving in the Seventh New Hampshire found life much like that of the men before them. Food was always a focus for soldiers. Calvin Shedd, a second lieutenant from Company A, wrote about the abundance of seafood: "We get Beef Mutton Clams Fish very cheap can buy Fish of 2 lbs for 5 cts the cheapest eating I have seen in the South there are plenty of Oysters for the getting & shelling I have had none as yet, for I don't know enough to open them." In a later letter to his family, he talked about the fruit available: "We have had plenty of oranges for 2 cts each…the rinds are green as grass, but quite good rather sour. I wish you could have some lemons, figs, peaches & many other fruits grow here. There are any quantity of sour oranges that any one can have by picking they are sour as lemons with a slight bitter taste, it is now out of season for most all fruits except oranges & lemons."[37]

Conditions for soldiers stationed at Fort Marion were not the best, however. First Sergeant Ferdinand Davis, from Lebanon, New Hampshire, related a funny story in his war remembrances of his time at Fort Marion:

> *But the intimate relationship to which each and every one was obliged to sustain to the hordes of fleas, flies, and rats was something human nature could not stand…My first night in these quarters was one of wakefulness. As soon as the lights were out rats, rats, long tailed rats came forth from their hiding places in squads, in platoons, companies and regiments. They deployed as skirmishers, assembled on the center, and right and left flanks. They advanced in heavy skirmish lines, in lines of battle, in massed columns, moved by the flanks and charged upon the center, till some tortured soul with an industrious flea on his right flank, enjoying a thanksgiving while another on the left is just getting down to work. Three good and hungry fellows are cavorting across his center and a whole hungry outfit like (___) are stealthily advancing along the spinal column determined to go for all there is in it. About this time the man awakes with an exclamation not found in the modern Sunday school book. He bounds from his bunk growing*

> *more and more sulphurious as he gets more awake; he seizes his rubber blanket (the only thing a man thinks of sleeping on under such conditions), makes his way to the entrance and gives it a vigorous shaking; gets back in his bunk and is fortunate to get asleep before the attack is resumed.*[38]

Calvin Shedd also wrote home about the flea problem: "The fleas are outrageous keep me awake nights. If there is anything that would make a Minister swear they will."[39]

With little to do, the men had to amuse themselves. Writing letters home was a common occurrence if paper was available, and the men liked to read and play games. When a boat was available, they would go out to fish and also watch for approaching vessels. Henry Little, the historian of the Seventh New Hampshire, relates that the men were able to get into a bit of trouble at times also. An old woman known only as Aunt Rhoda lived on the south side of town near the barracks and became the target of the young soldiers' practical jokes. One time, the men took a cow to the second floor of her home and removed the stairs so it was stuck. Another time, she came home and two pigs had been fastened inside her chimney flue. No mention was made as to how this was done or how the pigs were removed. It appears her complaints to Colonel Putnam fell on deaf ears.[40]

The New Hampshire boys spent both Thanksgiving and Christmas 1862 in St. Augustine. Thanksgiving was a time to remember those at home and was well put in a letter by Calvin Shedd: "How many times I have thought of you today & wished I might be with you. The Day has been very pleasant but cool. I have had some roast Pork & Pudding but have eaten the

An unidentified soldier from the Seventh New Hampshire Infantry. The Seventh New Hampshire served in St. Augustine from September through December 1862. *Courtesy State Archives of Florida.*

least I ever did at Thanksgiving." It was also a sad day, as related in the same letter:

> *This morning we had a sad accident here at the Fort culpably careless one of the guards forgetting for a moment that his piece was loaded in a playful manner raised it as if to fire & at the same time gave the command ready, aim, fire & he did fire & hit one of his comrades in the left breast the ball passing through his left lung within one 1½ inches of his heart, then passing through another man's wrist & hit another man's gun glancing from that to the breast of a corporal without injury as the ball was spent. The man shot through is not expected to live although he is at the time of writing. All the parties belong to God.*[11]

Christmas Eve was spent in church for many men: "On the 24th, passes were granted to all soldiers who wished to attend the midnight mass at the cathedral, and many of us availed ourselves of the opportunity."[12]

While much was calm, there could be danger, as the interior of Florida was controlled by Captain J.J. Dickison and his men. These Confederate guerrillas could make activities such as hunting and wood gathering dangerous for Union soldiers if not accompanied by enough armed men. On January 10, 1863, just such an event occurred as First Lieutenant Virgil H. Cate, Private Oscar F. French and sutler Samuel Riddell were captured while beyond Union picket lines. They had been hunting but were outnumbered by a guerrilla band. March 9, 1863, brought another skirmish with Dickison's men. Union pickets on the Jacksonville Road were confronted by Confederates, who drove them back to the main Union line. Four companies of Union troops were sent to combat the enemy. Three Confederates were taken prisoner, with five Union men from Company D being captured while on a flanking maneuver on the Palatka Road. No lives were lost.[13]

With the arrival of spring, the New Hampshire troops were relieved by the Seventh Connecticut and Colonel Joseph R. Hawley. For Henry Little, leaving this post was a sad event: "We regretted exceedingly to leave St. Augustine, for we had found its climate very agreeable, and our accommodations had been much better than could be furnished to troops in garrison, even in time of peace."[14]

Stephen Walkley, the historian of the Seventh Connecticut, stated that the main purpose for troops in St. Augustine was to feed and regulate the population. Walkley estimated that the population of the town was now only seven hundred whites and three hundred blacks. The time they spent in St. Augustine was called their easiest time in the war. A story is told that Colonel Hawley caught a thirty-three-pound bass while stationed in the city. The men were in town to celebrate the June 17 anniversary of the Battle of Bunker Hill. This was celebrated with a church meeting, speeches from Colonel Hawley and Lieutenants Dempsey and Wildman and music from the glee band. The Connecticut troops were not in Florida long before they were sent to Hilton Head and, later, to take part in the siege at Fort Wagner.[15]

Early August 1863 saw the arrival of the Forty-eighth New York Infantry under the command of Lieutenant Colonel Dudley W. Strickland. It had been sent to St. Augustine after having spent time in Georgia at Fort Pulaski. The regimental historian for the Forty-eighth described the city and its inhabitants much the same as men from prior regiments had: "The ancient houses were built of concrete, and the inhabitants were descendants from the early French and Spanish settlers. They were poor enough during the war, and many of them were allowed rations by the Government. Fruits, fish, sweet potatoes, and sweet milk were plentiful however, and very cheap." The soldiers were quartered at both Fort Marion and the St. Francis Barracks to the south, while some officers were allowed to room with loyal Unionists in the city such as Clarissa Anderson. The population of St. Augustine was estimated to be only four hundred, but no designation is made as to whether this is just the white population.

Lieutenant Colonel Dudley W. Strickland and the Forty-eighth New York spent only two months in St. Augustine but were well remembered for having brought a theater stage with them from Fort Pulaski, Georgia. *Courtesy Military Order of the Loyal Legion—Massachusetts Commandery (MOLLUS-MASS) Photograph Collection, United States Army Military History Institute.*

The Forty-eighth New York became a popular fixture in town because it brought with it the workings of a theater and formed the Barton Dramatic Association. The plays performed allowed residents and soldiers the chance to escape everyday life for a short while. Despite this fun, Provost Marshal James M. Nichols reported that pickets were occasionally fired upon, and he was sure that illicit communication between citizens and Confederate troops outside the city was taking place.[16]

Colonel Francis A. Osborne commanded the Twenty-fourth Massachusetts and Tenth Connecticut while they were stationed in St. Augustine. *Courtesy State Archives of Florida.*

By mid-October, the New Yorkers were ordered north, and the men from the Twenty-fourth Massachusetts and Tenth Connecticut arrived under the command of Colonel Francis A. Osborne. The fall of 1863 was a transition time both in the war and in St. Augustine. As the war became bloodier, St. Augustine became home to a Union hospital and convalescent camp. This helped put local men to work building and then women serving at the hospital. Local farmers were often able to sell any surplus produce to the hospital. Even though this helped support the Union war effort, many locals were in such dire straits that they did not seem to care.

Upon arrival, the men reported the town to be the same as those before them. According to Oliver Walker of the Twenty-fourth Massachusetts, "We have just as many oranges as we wish to eat, and are not slow to eat all that we can hold. We have the finest possible fish and oysters, and abundance of fresh vegetables, which are now just in season. I have been fishing twice; on last Thursday, I caught, among other fish, two very fine bass one weighing twelve, and the other ten pounds. Pretty good fishing I thought."[17]

Lieutenant Walker would find out, however, that all was not peaceful in Florida. Skirmishes with Confederate troops became a bit more regular as well. J.J. Dickison's men became more active in the area, and Union troops were on high alert when they ventured outside the walled city. In late December, Dickison set up an ambush for Union troops sent to cut wood. During the night, he had concealed his men along a roadway to wait for the anticipated workers. An advance guard of Union troops spotted the Confederates hiding in the palmettos lining the road. The Confederate leader demanded the surrender of the Union troops, but Lieutenant Walker ordered a Union attack. During the skirmish, several Union soldiers were killed and twenty-four taken prisoner. Lieutenant Oliver Walker was badly wounded and died in a St. Augustine hospital on January 3, 1864. An attempt by a large number of Union men to find Dickison's men proved fruitless, as the Confederates knew the land and also the locals.[18]

Men from the Tenth Connecticut reported things much the same as the Twenty-fourth Massachusetts did. James Linsley in his diary noted that one man was said to have picked 2,400 oranges from one tree. The value of this haul was seventy-two dollars. Corporal William Norton also commented on the abundant nature of oranges and on the many pretty Spanish girls. Private John Burnett, despite grumbling about the overall situation in the army, stated, "This is not much of a place now but it has been a fine place in its day."[19]

Henry Camp, of the Tenth Connecticut, served as first lieutenant while stationed in St. Augustine. In September 1864, he was promoted to major and was killed on October 13, 1864, at Darbytown Road, Virginia. *Courtesy the author.*

The Thanksgiving holiday for men of the Tenth Connecticut and Twenty-fourth Massachusetts was festive but sparse. Lieutenant James Linsley of the Tenth Connecticut reported that they had a turkey dinner and a service preached by Mr. Brinkenhoff. Afterward, there was a "Concert by Glee Club of an interesting character." William Norton, also of the Tenth Connecticut, stated, "Our Thanksgiving here was rather slim with less to eat that day than usual. They had a theatre down town in the P.M. and a concert in the evening."[50]

The year 1864 brought a celebration of the Emancipation Proclamation. James Linsley recorded it this way: "Addresses on the Plaza by Anti-Slavery men of New England to the negroes of this slave ridden state of Florida. Music by the colored schools who came out in procession in gala dress. Winding up with fine collation provided by the colored people, to which the army officers of both regiments and the hospital and others were invited."[51]

Henry Clay Trumbull served as chaplain for the Tenth Connecticut. After the war, Trumbull continued in his calling and for many years published the *Sunday School Times*, a religious journal. At the funeral of Ulysses S. Grant, he gave the prayer after the playing of Taps. *Courtesy Military Order of the Loyal Legion—Massachusetts Commandery (MOLLUS-MASS) Photograph Collection, United States Army Military History Institute.*

April 1864 brought the call for both regiments to leave St. Augustine and be replaced by the Seventeenth Connecticut. Having spent a restful time far from the front lines of battle, it was often difficult to motivate the men to leave knowing their lives would be in danger. Chaplain Henry Clay Trumbull of the Tenth Connecticut attempted to motivate the men in a sermon delivered on April 10, 1864, titled "Desirableness of Active Service."

In his sermon, Trumbull pushed the virtue of being fighting men:

> *The question should be with us of the Tenth, not what have we done but what can we do? It was truly said in a charity sermon that, as to our offerings, God looks not so much at what we have given as at what we have left. Our country is to be saved, under God, by hard fighting. Its best fighting men are needed now. Our regiment fights hard, fights well. Let it go forward! We did not leave our homes to avoid danger, to enjoy social life, to have an easy time. We came out to fight, to follow up the enemies of the government until they were all in subjection. The work is yet incomplete. We have strength left for it. Our enlistment still holds. The call comes to us. The way is open. Duty clearly points us on.*

Trumbull continued on, almost chiding the troops as having grown soft and weak in a location such as St. Augustine:

> *Active campaigning is as much better—for officers and men—than camp and garrison duty, as the latter is above the occupation of the mere money seekers or lovers of ease and security. Said a prominent General of our army—whom all knew to have felt the truth in his own experience—"The baptism of battle and of blood, makes men braver, nobler, holier." And it is so. A life of effort, a life of sacrifice, lifts men out of, and above themselves, as could no life of inaction or passive enjoyment of temporal advantages. In mental powers and physical ability, as in worldly goods, it is more blessed to give than to receive...But our regiment would suffer by remaining in such a place and life as now, longer than is necessary to recruit its health and prepare it for new and effective service at the front.*[52]

The words of the chaplain fell on some deaf ears, however, as recorded by diarist William Norton: "The Chaplain has been giving us a sermon on our duty, which he says is to go to the front and join our brethren in Va. We don't quite see the point. We have had glory enough without begging the privilege for more. His text was 'Shall ye sit here while your brethren go to war?' We rather think we shall, unless we get orders to go from higher authority than himself."[53]

A prolific letter writer, Private Justus A. Silliman of New Canaan, Connecticut, has provided researchers with many insights as to the locations and battles he participated in. *Courtesy New Canaan Historical Society.*

A higher authority did intervene. The Tenth Connecticut was sent to Gloucester Point, Virginia, and the Seventeenth Connecticut arrived in mid-April 1864. The election of 1864 had the potential to completely reshape the war effort. A victory by Republican Abraham Lincoln would continue the war as it was—a war to bring the Southern states back and also to free slaves in the states in rebellion. A win by Democratic candidate George McClellan had the potential to bring slaveholding states back into the Union and leave the status of slavery as it had been. Battlefield victories helped lead Lincoln to reelection. The Seventeenth Connecticut was solidly behind Lincoln, and according to Private Justus Silliman, McClellan received only fifteen votes from the regiments stationed in St. Augustine.

Holidays were always celebrated by the Seventeenth Connecticut, the first holiday being the Fourth of July, Independence Day. Captain Albert Peck recorded in his diary: "We had quite a nice celebration at St. Augustine. We had a national salute, reading of the Declaration of Independence, an oration and a good dinner. I was just well enough to ride down town from the hospital and witness the celebration." By Thanksgiving, Peck was stationed just west of St. Augustine in Picolata. Here he remembered, "Thanksgiving Day we had no meat for dinner so I took my gun and went up the river a mile or so and killed six nice ducks and I brought them home and our cook had them picked and roasted for dinner and we had a grand dinner."[54] Justus Silliman, of Company H, was stationed in Jacksonville on the Thanksgiving holiday and in a letter home recounted:

> *Thanksgiving has come and gone and I am glad of it as it was celebrated here by an unusual circulation of whiskey which caused much drunkenness though there was no serious disturbance. We did but little work on the day; I heard a short discourse from Mr. Swaim after which we adjourned to dinner which consisted of pork, potatoes, and an enormous "duff" (pudding) stuffed with raisins. I spent the afternoon in walking around seeing the sights & pitching quoits in which latter exercise I was very fortunate.*[55]

Christmas Eve brought word that Colonel William H. Noble had been taken prisoner while returning to St. Augustine from Jacksonville. Reports left by Silliman and Peck are similar in their description of events. Colonel Noble had been in Jacksonville testifying at a court-martial case and was returning to St. Augustine along with "Lieut. Rice, Asst. Pro. Marl. D.F. & Capt. Young just discharged from the service." The officers did not have an escort, nor were they carrying any weapons. About twenty miles from St.

Andersonville Prison, where Colonel Francis A. Noble was sent after capture, was arguably the worst of all Civil War prisoner of war camps. During the war, the prison held nearly forty-five thousand men in total; nearly thirteen thousand would perish, many due to malnutrition, diarrhea and the elements. *Courtesy Library of Congress.*

Augustine, in a swampy area, the buggy with the Union officers was stopped by two or three armed Confederates who demanded surrender. Having no arms, the colonel and his men did as told. Captain Young was allowed to continue on his way but without benefit of a horse.

Young arrived in St. Augustine with the bad news, and Major Allen was sent on horseback to alert the troops stationed at Picolata. Troops from St. Augustine patrolled the roads, and men from Picolata were ordered to patrol the St. Johns River in hopes of heading off the captors. Yet again, however, Confederate knowledge of the area proved vital, and the Union searches were in vain. Colonel Noble was first taken to Tallahassee and then imprisoned at Macon, Georgia, before being taken to the officers' quarters at Andersonville Prison. Colonel Noble was paroled on April 8, 1865. In March 1865, upon the recommendation of Ulysses S. Grant, Noble was commissioned a brevet brigadier general.[56]

April 1865 brought the highest of highs and the lowest of lows to the men of the Tenth Connecticut. Early April brought news of the surrender of Robert E. Lee and the Army of Northern Virginia. Albert Peck remembered, "We got the news of Lee's surrender the next day after it happened and our boys had quite a time celebrating. I was out fishing in the harbor when the news came with Burt Tomlinson and the guns began to fire at and around the fort and we soon pulled up our anchor and went in shore to see what was the matter." Justus Silliman in a letter to his mother stated, "It was not until the 17th just at evening that we received the Glorious news of the capture of Lee & his army. It was contained in the 'N.Y. Times' of the 10th inst. which was brought from Fernandina in a small boat…and when we first heard the news we were so overwhelmed with joy that we could not express it, but shook hands together, hugged each other and cut up all sorts of antics in our ecstacy."

The joy of victory was short-lived, however, as news of the assassination of Abraham Lincoln quickly made its way to Florida. On April 24, a saddened Private Silliman wrote to his brother:

> *We received the sad and startling intelligence of the assassination of President Lincoln and Secretary Seward, last Saturday night while we were rejoicing over the glorious news of the recent victory of our arms, and the prospects of speedy peace and restoration of the union. So great was our surprise and grief on hearing it that we could not utter a word. It seemed as though from the sunshine of our joy we had become suddenly enveloped in a dark and gloomy cloud that was horrible to contemplate.*

Captain Peck was much more restrained in his comments: "In just three days after the news of Lee's surrender arrived at St. Augustine a vessel came into St. Augustine with her flag at half-mast announcing the assassination of President Lincoln and what a sad day that was for all of us."[57]

In early June 1865, the regiment was moved to Jacksonville, in early July it was in Hilton Head and on July 19 the Seventeenth Connecticut was mustered out of service.

The postwar economy was slow to pick up. Matthias Andreu attempted to restart publication of his newspaper, the *Examiner*, but met with limited success. A lack of hard capital held back many businessmen who were oftentimes unable to stock their shelves. Historian Thomas Graham has pointed out that many businesses did not even have proper signage announcing their stores.[58]

Soldiers who had been stationed in the state many times came back, with some settling in St. Augustine. These families brought a level of economic security to the region. Some of these men, such as George Greeno from

As military commander of Florida after the war, John T. Sprague moved the military headquarters from Tallahassee to St. Augustine. This change helped bring a sense of normalcy to the area and helped St. Augustine begin to recover economically from the hardships of war. *Courtesy State Archives of Florida.*

Derby, New Hampshire, who had served in the Fourth New Hampshire Company I, became active in local politics. Greeno was to serve four terms as mayor of St. Augustine.

Military rule in Florida arrived in March 1867 to mixed opinions. Many, of course, viewed it as northern aggression and revenge, while some were more accepting and cooperative. John T. Sprague was named as commander of the District of Florida. Sprague moved the army's headquarters from Tallahassee to St. Augustine, much to the delight of local businesses. The federal government and the soldiers stationed in the city spent a large amount of money. This helped put residents to work and helped bring needed goods to town. By 1870, though, the population of St. Augustine was still lower than it had been in 1830.

The military presence in St. Augustine worked in other ways as well. With the army in town, things tended to stay peaceful. The political turmoil and violence that occurred elsewhere were largely absent in St. Augustine. On occasion, there would be skirmishes between army members and local residents. In July 1868, Jacob Mickler shot and killed two soldiers who were stealing watermelons during the night. Mickler, who had fired deer slugs rather than birdshot, was arrested by the army but was never charged and was subsequently released.

The presence of the army also assured black residents that they would be allowed to register and vote. Despite their newly won freedoms, the

Democratic Party still dominated St. Augustine politics due to low black population in the city at the time. It is true, however, that black electoral participation was strong and helped launch several blacks into office during the 1870s and early 1880s.[59]

As the federal government began to back away from Reconstruction, blacks began to again suffer at the hands of conservative white governments. This was accomplished in Florida by a poll tax and other voting requirements. In an attempt to limit black political influence, the city was divided into various wards, with black neighborhoods being lumped together into a single ward. This system helped nullify the votes of those blacks who were still legally eligible to vote. The majority of black citizens were now free, but true freedom would still be seventy years away when Martin Luther King Jr. and others would use the 400th anniversary of the founding of St. Augustine as a platform to showcase the racial inequalities prevalent in the nation's oldest city.

Chapter 3

THE *JEFFERSON DAVIS*

The story of the *Jefferson Davis* is an interesting one starting well before the Civil War but lasting a very short time once the war started. Despite the fact that the ship was already out of commission by the end of the summer of 1861, the ship and its crew had earned a reputation as fierce privateers. Serving as a privateer for only two months, the ship captured and destroyed eight vessels.

Built in 1845 in Baltimore, the *Jefferson Davis* was originally christened the *Putnam* and sailed from New Orleans as a merchant ship. By the late 1850s, she had been renamed *Echo* and was being used to bring illegal slaves from Africa. In August 1858, she was located just north of Cuba, and her movements attracted attention from the United States ship *Dolphin*. Under command of Lieutenant John Newland Maffitt, the *Dolphin* gave chase, eventually raising the English flag and firing shots over the bow of the *Echo*. Upon seeing the United States flag raised by the *Echo*, the crew of the *Dolphin* raised her true colors.

Upon boarding the *Echo*, she was found to be nationless but carrying a large number of Africans, mostly naked and separated by sex. The number of Africans on board range from about 270 up to 450 depending on the source. The ship and her human cargo were taken to Charleston, South Carolina, where the Africans were transferred to the USS *Niagara* for a return voyage that saw them taken to the colony of Liberia. At trial, the *Echo* was declared forfeited and thus was to be sold at public auction. In January 1859, the *Echo* was purchased by Robert Hunter, a Charleston shipping merchant. He again named the ship *Putnam*.

The *Putnam* was short-lived, however, as soon thereafter, Confederate president Jefferson Davis issued a proclamation inviting ship owners to apply for letters of marque. A letter of marque was a government authorization for private ship owners to attack, capture, pillage and destroy enemy vessels—in this case, Union shipping vessels. As opposed to outright piracy, these were "state-sponsored pirates," as Ron Soodalter has called them.

Hunter was quick to bring aboard investors in his ship, including Louis M. Coxetter, and applied for a letter of marque. He proposed changing the name of his ship to *Rattlesnake*. Before receiving their commission on June 18, 1861, the owners agreed to change the name to the *Jefferson Davis*.

With letter in hand, the owners and crew hurriedly worked to finish overhauling and arming the ship. This proved to be difficult, and they were able to obtain only "five obsolete guns, old iron pieces made in England in 1801. Four of these, two 24-pounders and two short 32-pounders, were mounted in broadside, and a long 18-pounder was pivoted amidships. The armory was well stocked with double-barreled shotguns, muskets, cutlasses and revolvers." With crew and arms ready, the 187-ton *Jefferson Davis* set sail on June 28 with Captain Louis M. Coxetter at the helm.[60]

Louis M. Coxetter was no stranger to the people of St. Augustine. Coxetter was born in 1818 in Nova Scotia, Canada. His family moved to Charleston, where his career with the sea began. By 1841, he owned his own ship, the packet schooner *Stephen and Frances*, with which he made regular passage between Charleston and St. Augustine. In July 1841, he had taken an ad in the local paper stating:

> *The undersigned takes pleasure in informing the citizens of St. Augustine and the Public general, that he has newly fitted up the above vessel in a superior manner for the accommodation of Passengers, having added to her former conveniences an extensive and airy cabin on deck, with state rooms; and hopes by strict attention to his business, to receive such share of the public patronage as his merits shall deserve.*
>
> *Freight and passengers taken on as reasonable terms as by any other vessel.*
>
> *July 2, 1841.* *Louis Coxetter.*[61]

It was during his stays in St. Augustine that he met Antonica Geiger, the daughter of John and Ana Maria Geiger. They were married on July 1, 1845, at St. John's Episcopal Church in St. Augustine. At this time, Coxetter and family lived in a house on St. George Street that Antonica had inherited from her parents. The young couple appear to have had four sons: Louis

Jr., James, Sydney (who does not appear to live to adulthood) and Fernando (possibly known as Ferdinand).

The Coxetter fortunes were looking up at this point. Despite having lost the *Stephen and Frances* during the Mexican War, Louis landed on his feet. He began a partnership with J.W. Caldwell, and in 1851, the Florida Steam Packet Company was born. Coxetter then traveled to New York to personally supervise the building of the *Florida*, their first ship. By January 1852, the ship was operational and made her first journey on the St. Johns River. The owners took out local ads touting the new ship and L.M. Coxetter as master: "The *Florida* has been built under the superintendence of Captain Coxetter, and her speed and accommodations for passengers are unsurpassed by any boat ever placed on the St. John's. Freight and passage as low as by any other line."

The early 1850s were a successful time for the Florida Steam Packet Company and for Coxetter. By late 1851, he was successful enough to own slaves, as is evidenced by an ad he placed in a local paper when one ran away:

> *25 DOLLARS Will be paid as a reward, to any person who will apprehend and contain (so that I can obtain possession of her;) either in St. Johns or Duval County jail; my negro woman HANNAH:—She is of rather tall and slim make and of very erect carriage—of black complexion and between the ages of Forty-five and Fifty—She ran away from my family in St. Augustine, about the last of October or first of November 1851—and is supposed to be secreted, somewhere in the vicinity of the City.*[62]

Business was also looking good, and Coxetter had given command of the *Florida* to another captain and had returned north to purchase a second steamer, the *Carolina*. He commanded her for three years before leaving the Florida Steam Packet Company to form his own concern with the *Everglade* as his ship. Going into business for himself necessitated moving to Charleston, so the St. George Street home was sold. By 1860, however, competition had grown, and Coxetter was driven out of business. The *Everglade* was auctioned to pay off debts. Thus, Coxetter briefly found himself unemployed before joining Hunter and the *Jefferson Davis*.

On the evening of June 28, 1861, the *Jefferson Davis* and her crew left the Port of Charleston through Maffit's Channel and "not-withstanding the very efficient blockade of *Abraham I*" easily made her way into the Atlantic Ocean, turning north in search of merchant vessels. Her appearance was such that she could fool others into thinking she was a foreign ship:

> *The brig looks more like a foreign vessel than an American. The sails are of hemp, instead of the snowy staple of the Southland, and have a deep reach. The clews are cut sharp. There is but little rake to the masts. She has a square stern and a billet-head; and is black—mast-heads, yards, and hull. Her pivot gun is visible above the rail, and on the topgallant forecastle the funnel has a wooden cover which gives to it the semblance of a bow-chaser. The cabin is half under and half above deck. There is a boat on each quarter, and a number of studdingsail booms are lashed across the stern. She wears a rusty but nonchalant air as though having been long at sea upon a secret and satisfying mission: she in character. She probably registers a little less than two hundred tons and draws about twelve feet of water.*[63]

Her crew included another man with strong ties to St. Augustine: William Baya. He was born in St. Augustine in 1834 to parents Jose and Catherine Baya. Baya has been described as being approximately five feet, eight inches tall with dark complexion, hazel eyes and black hair. After his stint aboard the *Jefferson Davis*, he returned to St. Augustine in late 1861. He joined a company that was to become Company D Eighth Florida Infantry, in which he was elected captain. He led the Eighth Florida at Antietam. After being wounded, captured and exchanged at Fredericksburg, Baya was promoted to lieutenant colonel in January 1863. During the Battle of Gettysburg, he led the Eighth Florida during the infamous Pickett's Charge. He was severely wounded in the hip at Bristoe Station in 1863 and taken prisoner at Sailor's Creek in April 1865 before being detained at Johnson's Island, Ohio. He was released after taking the oath of allegiance in July. In addition to William, many of his family members also served in the Confederacy. William's uncle Francis Baya perished in a Union prisoner of war camp, and his name is carved on the Confederate Memorial that stands in the Plaza in downtown St. Augustine.

After the war, William moved to Jacksonville, where in 1866 he married Cornelia Canova. He was successful in the grocery business and was eventually elected an alderman of the city. He also held the title of brigadier general of the Florida State Militia. The Confederacy seems to have never been far from William's heart, however, as he served as commander of the R.E. Lee Camp number 58 of Jacksonville in the Sons of Confederate Veterans (SCV). He also served as brigadier general of the SCV. His wife, Cornelia, was an early member of the Martha Reid Chapter 19 of the United Daughters of the Confederacy. This was the first UDC chapter in the state of Florida.[64]

Almost immediately, the *Jefferson Davis* began spotting potential targets. On her second day at sea, three separate ships were spotted. None was chased due to problems on board. In addition, the third ship appeared to be French in nationality and was not considered a target. Several long days then passed without contact. On July 4, 1861, Captain Coxetter rallied his men, bringing them back to life with the help of a little bit of alcohol. This raising of spirits seemed to turn their fortune, as later that day two ships were spotted. One turned out to be British and the second from Maryland, so both were allowed to continue on.

On the morning of July 6, a target was spotted and captured. The *John Welsh* out of Philadelphia was found to be carrying a cargo of 273 hogsheads, 54 tierces and 286 barrels of muscovado sugar and 436 boxes of clayed sugar. She was sent to Charleston, by way of Savannah, and was sold at auction under order of the Charleston Prize Court.

Later that same day, Coxetter and crew made the fateful capture of the *Enchantress*, a Boston-based schooner cruising to Cuba with a load of supplies under the command of Captain Devereux. A crew under command of William Wallace Smith boarded the *Enchantress*, intending to take her to Savannah for future sale. Before leaving, needed supplies were transferred, and many of the crew were also sent to the *Jefferson Davis.* An exception was the schooner's cook, Jacob Garrick, a black man, who was not welcomed aboard by Coxetter.

For two weeks, Garrick faithfully continued his duties as cook. On July 22, they were met by the steamer USS *Albatross.* When Smith and crew tried to pass off that the *Enchantress* was still bound for Cuba, Garrick sprang into action. He jumped overboard, "singing out that it was 'a captured vessel of the privateer *Jeff. Davis* and they are taking her into Charleston.' I sang it out so that they could hear me on board the steamer." After being rescued from the waters of the Atlantic, Garrick was also able to testify that the privateers were calculating ways to impersonate the actual crew of the *Enchantress.* Each was assigned the name of a real crew member, and when they came up a man short, it was agreed they would claim he had been washed overboard. Upon Garrick's word, the men from the *Jefferson Davis* were taken to Philadelphia Naval Yard, where they were charged with piracy and removed to Moyamensing Prison.

The following day, July 7, the *S.J. Waring* was captured on its way to Montevideo. Despite reports to the contrary, the crew of the *S.J. Waring* found Captain Coxetter and crew to be quite accommodating: "We expected from the statements made in the New York papers, that we would be stripped of

Completed in 1835, Moyamensing Prison in Philadelphia was originally built to house four hundred inmates in addition to a debtors' prison. With law changes, the debtors' prison was converted to house female inmates. The prison was demolished in 1968. Stereoview by Alfred S. Campbell, Elizabeth, New Jersey. *Courtesy Library of Congress.*

everything and treated with the greatest severity; but our treatment was entirely different from that which we expected. Each officer did all in his power to make us comfortable."[65]

While the crew of the *S.J. Waring* may have been made comfortable aboard the *Jefferson Davis*, the same cannot be said for the privateers placed aboard the *S.J. Waring* in order to take her to port. In all, there were five men put aboard the *S.J. Waring* to act as a prize crew: prize master Mantague Amiel, Seamen George Stephens and Malcolm Liddy and privateersmen Milnor and Smith. Just as was the case with the *Enchantress*, a black cook was left aboard the ship. His name was William Tillman. Tillman was a strong man and stood just short of six feet tall. In his role as cook, Tillman was given extraordinary freedom, especially considering he was technically a prisoner.

After being at sea under the charge of prize master Amiel for more than a week, the ship neared Charleston Harbor. All three officers were asleep in their bunks, and the two privateersmen appear to have not been on duty. Tillman spotted his opportunity and sprang into action. Using his superior size, and also an axe, he was able to kill the three officers, tossing their bodies overboard to a watery grave. He then took command of the vessel and, despite having no experience commanding a ship, was able to navigate his way north and into New York's Hudson River, arriving on July 21. While given a hero's welcome, Tillman was held until the official investigation was completed. He was then released and was later employed by P.T. Barnum. It was said that he carried his bloody axe and the ship's flag as he retold his story to those in attendance at Barnum's events. William Tillman was to

William Tillman was serving as a cook aboard the *S.J. Waring* when it was captured by the *Jefferson Davis*. While en route to a Confederate port, Tillman killed the Confederate crew and sailed the ship to a Union port. For his deeds, Tillman was rewarded with a portion of the ship's bounty. This engraving originally appeared in an 1861 issue of *Harper's Weekly*. *Courtesy U.S. Naval Historical Center.*

later receive a $7,000 share of the salvage money that was awarded by the District Court for the Southern District of New York.[66]

Coxetter knew nothing of the events aboard the *S.J. Waring* and continued along. On July 9, both the *Mary Goodell* and the *Mary E. Thompson* were overtaken, but neither was seized, as they were not considered valuable enough. The only item that appears to have been taken from the ships was fresh water. In fact, Coxetter loaded prisoners from earlier captures on board both vessels and allowed them to go free rather than destroying them based on their word that they would continue toward their original destinations. The ship captains, of course, did no such thing and quickly headed to Union ports in order to alert others to the proximity of the privateer. This lapse in judgment by Coxetter allowed Union warships to know he was in the area and to begin hunting for him.

On July 21, Captain Coxetter and crew captured what they thought would be a valuable ship, the *Alvarado*, on its way from South Africa to Boston, loaded with wool, sheepskins, copper and iron. Together, the ship and cargo were estimated to be worth nearly $100,000. The prize was sent south under the command of Gilbert Hay. Unfortunately for the privateers, Hay seems to have lost his nerve when faced with the Union warship *Jamestown* near the entrance of the St. Mary's River near Amelia Island. It was here that he ran the *Alvarado* aground, forcing his men to make a hasty retreat to the coast and safety. Despite artillery fire from Confederates, the *Jamestown*'s commander, Charles Green, sent a party aboard who removed the ship's papers and the journal of the ship captain's wife before then setting fire to the grounded vessel. The whole event seems to have been quite a piece of entertainment for those on shore, as a letter from Norman Brownson indicates:

> *The Privateer* Jeff. Davis *(Capt. Coxetter) is driving a brisk business, yesterday our town was in a very great state of excitement, early in the morning a few of us went to the top of Dr. Clay's house to take a look at the blockading vessels which are seen almost every day, sometimes very near the bar and then disappearing evidently on the look for privateers and their* [?]. *As we got to the top of the house we discovered two vessels one a little north east of the bar and out some way from the bar, the other was south from the bar a little south of center street and nearer the coast and seemed to have all sail set and making for the coast with a stiff breeze. It was not long before the house top was covered, all anxious to get a sight at the vessels through a glass. As the vessel at the south kept on her course, all made up their minds that one was a prize vessel endeavoring to make the bar and the other was* Old Abe *in pursuit, and the one to the south must be the prize, and was making for the beach as she could not make the bar soon the drums began to beat, the different companies got under march for the beach. The artillery with two cannon.*[67]

By this time, the *Jefferson Davis* was running low on officers who could take control of a prize ship. August 5, however, turned out to be a strong day for the crew and one that Coxetter could not let go. The crew first captured the schooner *Windward* and its load of salt. Then a bigger prize came into view: the *Santa Clara*. The *Santa Clara* was loaded down with sugars, molasses, furniture and other valuable cargo. Not having an officer to take the ship to port, Coxetter appointed a prize crew with the ranking officer being a helmsman. He chose wisely though, and the ship made it safely to Savannah, where the cargo was auctioned for top dollar. The ship itself was seized by the Confederate government and sunk in the Savannah River to act as a

The USS *Jamestown* intercepted the *Alvarado*, a ship captured by the *Jefferson Davis*, and burned her near the entrance to the St. Mary's River. *Courtesy Library of Congress.*

barricade. The *Windward* was eventually released, albeit now loaded with her crew plus the crews of the *Alvarado* and the *Santa Clara*.

Coxetter was now desperately short of men, food and water. His plan was to dock in St. Augustine and replenish everything. The entry to St. Augustine contains a difficult-to-navigate bar, and with the winds being tricky, Coxetter tried to wait out the elements. On August 18, the *Jefferson Davis* ran aground. Locals took boats out to save what they could, including the crew. When the men arrived in town, they were given a hero's welcome, including a ringing of church bells.

The men did not stay in St. Augustine for long, however. Soon they were on to other adventures, some earning more fame than others. Captain Coxetter and Lieutenant Postell stayed in the marine field and both captained blockade runners for the rest of the war. The previously mentioned William Baya earned promotions in the Confederate army to the rank of lieutenant colonel and led a regiment during Pickett's Charge at Gettysburg. A helmsmen named J.F. Carlsen, a European immigrant, achieved lasting fame due to his having perished while aboard the *H.L. Hunley*. After having

The USS *Housatonic* was responsible for the sinking of the Confederate submarine the *H.L. Hunley*. Original art by William Waud. *Courtesy Library of Congress.*

served in the artillery division, earning an award for bravery at the Battle of Fort Walker, Carlsen volunteered to serve aboard the still-new submarine. Carlsen was assigned the dangerous position of fourth crank handle. During the battle with the USS *Housatonic* on February 17, 1864, the *H.L. Hunley* was sunk, and all aboard perished.[68]

The legend of the *Jefferson Davis* is really bigger than the actual deeds she and her crew accomplished. This was still early in the war, and both sides were clinging to any hope that it would be a short one. Looking back after 150 years, it is easy to see that the *Jefferson Davis* did not accomplish a lot that would hurt the Union or any of its states. She captured and destroyed fewer than a dozen ships, none vital to the Union war effort. However, at the time, the *Charleston Mercury* may have said it best: "The name of the privateer *Jefferson Davis* has become a word of terror to the Yankees."[69]

Chapter 4

Abraham Lincoln Associations

Abraham Lincoln never had a chance to visit Florida, let alone the city of St. Augustine. In fact, he did not receive any recorded votes in the state during the 1860 presidential election. Florida overwhelmingly put its support behind the Southern Democratic Party candidate, John Breckinridge. Breckinridge beat out John Bell and his running mate, Edward Everett—who later was the keynote speaker at the Gettysburg National Cemetery dedication on the day Lincoln made perhaps the most famous speech of all time—by a margin of over 8,000 votes to right around 4,800. This victory gave him the state's three electoral votes. Democrat and longtime Lincoln opponent Stephen A. Douglas polled fewer than 400 votes, with the actual number varying depending on the source. Despite coming in second in the national popular vote, Douglas was able to secure victory in only two states and finished a distant fourth in electoral votes.

A potential reason for Douglas's poor showing in the South and particularly Florida has been put forth by John F. Reiger. Reiger believes that voters may have been scared off by Douglas's espousing the Freeport Doctrine. The Freeport Doctrine, while having been laid out prior, famously came about during the second Lincoln-Douglas debate, which occurred on August 27, 1858, in Freeport, Illinois. The doctrine essentially said that no matter what the United States Supreme Court ruled, the people of a state or territory had the right to decide whether to be "free" or "slave." This type of rhetoric scared those of the slaveholding class who demanded full protection of what they considered to be their right to own slaves. Reiger takes his theory a step further in suggesting that the votes Douglas did receive in the state probably came from transplanted anti-slave Northerners.[70]

Mary Lincoln

Mary Todd Lincoln, the widow of President Abraham Lincoln, briefly spent time in St. Augustine at the home of John Francis Whitney. Original photograph by Mathew B. Brady. *Courtesy Library of Congress.*

While Abraham Lincoln did not visit the state, his widow, Mary Todd Lincoln, did and was a visitor to the St. Augustine area during the winter of 1874–75. Little is known about Mrs. Lincoln's time in St. Augustine. While in town, she stayed with the family of John Francis Whitney. In a family record, Mr. Whitney wrote, "Mrs. Lincoln, widow of President Lincoln, was a guest at my home at Ravenswood, Florida, winter of 1874. Spent a week with us."[71]

Mr. Whitney was a man of wealth; he was a grandson of Eli Whitney, the inventor of the cotton gin. John and his family were early promoters of St. Augustine as a tourist destination. John was born in Massachusetts and eventually got into the publishing industry. He was a backer of the *Boston Herald* and established the *New York Pathfinder*. He later served a term as mayor of Rahway, New Jersey, before moving to St. Augustine. In Florida, he continued in the publishing industry, operating the *St. Augustine Press* and the *Florida Weekly*. He was also involved in real estate development. The Whitneys purchased a large tract of land west of the San Sebastian River that included the island today known as Spengler Island, on which they built a large home.

They called the land Ravenswood and intended to sell off smaller parcels, hoping to attract other wealthy northerners. Mr. Whitney opened the first Fountain of Youth in St. Augustine and also operated an alligator farm on the Ravenswood property.

The Whitney family fortunes changed sometime just before the turn of the century. In 1899, their island was sold to Dennis Sweeney by First National Bank. The 1900 U.S. Federal Census shows John and his wife, Maria, whom he had been married to since 1846, living in Vernon, Vermont. By 1902, however, the Whitneys were back in St. Augustine, where they would both live out their last days. John passed away in 1902 and Maria soon thereafter in 1904. Both are buried in Evergreen Cemetery in St. Augustine.[72]

Mary Lincoln herself left little evidence of her time in St. Augustine. It appears there is only one known letter from her during her stay. While in St. Augustine on February 20, 1875, she wrote to a Mrs. Bradwell about her time in Florida, her physical and mental state and the difficulty of travel:

> *And, I have so often wished that we could be together in this "Sunny clime." I am now looking down upon a yard with its roses, white lilacs, and other flowers. (Although it is raining and we have had a good deal of rain in its soft, dreamy, light fashion,) since the middle of January, I remained too much out, on my balcony, took a severe cold, had much inward and outward fever for three weeks and one day when it was raging at its height I told my nurse to pack up a small trunk and valise and we would leave town. So, on the 11th of Feb. we started for this place five hours distant from Jacksonville by boat and railway. On board the steamer I met three or four choice Philadelphia friends, ladies and gentlemen and they insisted upon my joining them and instead of a modest journey of five hours to St. A. it proved four days and nights on the boat. If these comme il faut*[73] *persons from the north generally and the most charming scenery on the celebrated Ocklawahs river*[74] *could give pleasure, then it certainly was mine. Words would fail in description going from the broad St. John's into the narrow streams. With scenery such as is seldom met with in this world such pens as W.C. Bryant and others have given minute details of the voyage. Scribner's November monthly speaks of it and Harper dwells at great length upon it. How much we will have to say to each other when we meet. From this most unexpected excursion I came here. I have been here five days, three of which have been passed in bed. For you may be well assured that the fever in my veins, must run its course. But two bright days I have emerged from it wandering over this quaint and most interesting place. My first visit was of course to the*

> *ancient Fort and my wondering head was in every prison nook until we came to the one whose entrance was excavated I believe in 1835, where two iron cages were found, one, now said to be in the Smithsonian Institute at Wash. Hooked to the wall, where history records, and the Sergeant repeats, the story that two prisoners were enclosed in these same cages walled in, left to their fate, with God alone to be merciful to them! The prison of course is in darkness except the dim light held by the sergeant. I entered the fearful place and how I came out of it and how I have suffered in mind since our merciful Heavenly Father alone knows the wrongs of time will be redressed in a brighter world! My son writes that the winter has been terribly cold and my good friend and your dear husband, how is he getting along and how is his health this winter?*[75]

JOHN HAY

One of those closest to Lincoln during his time in the White House was personal secretary John Hay. Hay was born in Salem, Indiana, in October 1838. Hay's uncle Milton operated his law office next door to that of Abraham Lincoln, so Lincoln was already familiar with the young man before winning the presidential election. Once elected, Lincoln's secretary John Nicolay recommended that the young Hay be hired as an assistant. During the Lincoln administration, Hay lived in the White House, sharing a second-floor room with Nicolay. Hay stayed with Lincoln until the end and was in attendance when Lincoln died. His long career in governmental work would be broken only by a stint as editor for the *New York Tribune* in the 1870s. Hay returned to politics in 1878 after being named assistant secretary of state under President Hayes and later serving as ambassador to the United Kingdom. In 1898, Hay became secretary of state under President Taft, a position he would continue to hold under Theodore Roosevelt until his death in July 1905.

In 1863, Hay spent several months away from his White House duties. He was to spend time carrying news and orders to Samuel DuPont, the admiral who was making plans to attack Charleston, South Carolina. Hay did not enlist in the army or navy but rather served as a volunteer aide-de-camp to General David Hunter in Hilton Head. And while Hay proclaimed to have been what could be called burned out, it seems he had other motives as well. His brother Lieutenant Charles Hay served on Hunter's staff, thus allowing them to have a family reunion of sorts. Hay was also of prime enlistment and draft age, and based on what he told John Nicolay, he did not want to be seen as shirking his duty: "I want my abolition record clearly defined and that will do it better than anything else, in my own mind and the minds of a few dozen people we know."

John Hay served as a personal secretary to President Abraham Lincoln and later served as secretary of state under Presidents Rutherford B. Hayes and Theodore Roosevelt. *Courtesy Library of Congress.*

John Hay arrived in Hilton Head on April 7, only a few hours before the disastrous attack on Fort Sumter. The Union navy was badly outgunned that day, and Admiral Samuel F. DuPont withdrew his forces. Hay wrote Lincoln a letter outlining the failure but hoped that despite the loss, the men could still be treated with honor due to their bravery.

What should have been a happy reunion with his brother turned out to be a difficult time for Hay due to the Union loss but also because he found Charles sick with pneumonia. Despite having to care for his sick brother, John found time to be active on Hunter's staff, taking part on inspection tours along the coasts of South Carolina and Georgia.

Charles's condition was not improving, and his doctor suggested sea air might help in clearing his lungs. The brothers traveled south by boat, ending up in St. Augustine. It was here that John found what he considered to be a paradise, as he wrote to John Nicolay: "It is the only thing that smells of the Original Eden on the Continent. I wish I could buy the State for taxes & keep it for the Castle of Indolence." It was during this trip that Hay decided to invest in Florida real estate. With men being out of town fighting for the Confederacy, many times their land was sold by Union-appointed tax collectors. Hay made arrangements to purchase an orange grove for $500. He was confident of his investment, writing his grandfather, "The soil is almost as rich as our prairie land. All sorts of fruit and grain grow with very little cultivation, and fish and game of every kind abound." As they headed back toward Hilton Head, with Charles still convalescing, John bought more land in Fernandina.

In January 1864, Abraham Lincoln sent Hay to Florida in support of his new 10 Percent Plan. The 10 Percent Plan would allow a state currently in rebellion to be readmitted to the Union under two conditions, the first being that 10 percent of the citizens, based on 1860 populations, must take an oath of allegiance to the Union. The second condition was emancipation of all slaves.

Union major general Quincy A. Gilmore served as commanding general of the Army of the South. He is most known for his success at Fort Pulaski and failure at Fort Wagner. Troops under his command were also repulsed at the Battle of Olustee near Tallahassee, Florida. *Courtesy Library of Congress.*

Lincoln made sure to give Hay the opportunity for success and commissioned him a major in the army and assigned him the position of assistant adjutant general reporting to Major General Quincy Adams Gillmore, who was serving as commander of the Army of the South. At the time, Gillmore was preparing for an offensive in Florida that was ultimately to be the Battle of Olustee, a glaring Federal defeat.

Hay's visit was looked at with skepticism by many. Lincoln critics saw this plan as an attempt to bolster his sagging reelection prospects. If Florida rejoined the Union, it would have been likely that Lincoln would have received Florida's three electoral votes at the upcoming

Republican Convention. While many questioned Lincoln, there were others who questioned Hay and his motives. It was widely known that Hay had dealings with Lyman Stickney. Stickney was the Federal tax commissioner who convinced Hay to invest in Florida real estate. Stickney had connections with Secretary of the Treasury Salmon P. Chase, and both he and Hay stood to gain financially and politically from a reconstructed Florida.

The efforts made by Hay proved ineffectual. Despite spending time in Fernandina, Jacksonville, St. Augustine and Key West, there was little interest by the citizens of the state: "The people of the interior would be indignant against such a snap-judgment taken by incomers & would be jealous and sullen." Hay returned to Washington, having failed to garner 10 percent of the population as mandated. He also was considered partly to blame for the loss at Olustee. The *New York Herald* bluntly stated, "It is rumored that the expedition was intended simply for the occupation of Florida for the purpose of securing the election of three Lincoln delegates to the National Nominating Convention, and that of John Hay to Congress." In regards to the loss of life at Olustee, it continued, "The President and his secretary are the only ones to blame in the business."

During the war years, Henry Shelton Sanford served as ambassador to Belgium and later helped found the city of Sanford, Florida. Original photograph by Mathew B. Brady. *Courtesy Library of Congress.*

The loss at Olustee and the failure of the 10 Percent Plan led to a personal loss for Hay as well. With the turmoil of the war still going and the postwar uncertainty of Reconstruction, Hay was never able to take possession of the real estate he had purchased. After the war, he quickly sold his St. Augustine grove to Henry Shelton Sanford, who was later to become the founder of the Florida town of Sanford, near present-day Orlando. Both Hay's investment and time in Florida had come to an end.[76]

ULYSSES S. GRANT

Despite a prior reputation for drunkenness and a sometimes spotty record, Ulysses S. Grant rose to command the Union army and is considered by many still to this day to be the savior of the Union. In late 1863, Lincoln promoted Grant to be in charge of all Union armies, a move that while proving deadly for thousands of soldiers ultimately led to the defeat of Robert E. Lee's troops and eventually the surrender of the last vestiges of the Confederate army.

Grant had become such a hero and was held in such esteem by the president that Lincoln invited Grant and his wife, Julia, to be his guests at Ford's Theater on the night of April 14, 1865. This is, of course, the night that John Wilkes Booth shot Lincoln and grievously wounded Lincoln's eventual guest, Major Henry Rathbone. This event has led to one of the great "what ifs" in history. Would things have turned out differently if Grant had accepted Lincoln's invitation?

Grant later served two terms as president of the United States from 1869 to 1877. While the Grant administration had successes such as the Treaty of Washington in 1871, the creation of the Department of Justice and many efforts to protect the rights of black citizens during the Reconstruction era, his terms were not without scandal. Issues with appointees during his term led to events such as the Sanborn Contract, the Whiskey Ring, the Trading Post Ring and others that left a stain on the administration that was not easily washed away.

After leaving office, the Grants embarked on a world tour, taking them to locales such as Europe, Russia, Egypt, Israel, China, Japan and Taiwan. The trip was a huge success, and many in the Republican Party wanted to use this as a springboard to another presidential bid. This ultimately proved unsuccessful, however, and he lost the 1880 nomination to James Garfield.

Grant's connection to St. Augustine begins with his wife, Julia Boggs Dent. Julia was the sister of Frederick Tracy Dent, who as brevet brigadier general was appointed commander of troops at St. Francis Barracks in St. Augustine. It has been said that General Dent made two requests to his sister regarding her husband. Dent's first request was for funding in order to build officers' quarters at the St. Francis Barracks. After funds were approved, drawings were made up in 1882, and construction began shortly thereafter. The style of the quarters is reminiscent of those at the Carlisle Barracks in Pennsylvania.

The second request made by Frederick Dent was for his sister and President Grant to visit St. Augustine during their tour of the world. The

Grants arrived back in the United States in September 1879. By January 1880, they were traveling again, with plans to visit Florida, Cuba and then Mexico.[77] The Grants first arrived in Florida on January 4, 1880, at the train station in Fernandina. They stayed for nearly two weeks in the area, seeing Fernandina, Jacksonville, Oak Park and other cities.

Our knowledge of Grant's visit to St. Augustine is through the efforts of Holmes Ammidown. Ammidown and his family were winter visitors to the city from the mid-1850s through the 1920s, preferring the mild Florida temperatures to the cold of Massachusetts. Writing was an avocation for Ammidown, and he often submitted articles to newspapers both local and near his northern home. In 1866, he began keeping scrapbooks of these writings that he titled "Miscellaneous Writings by Holmes Ammidown, Contributed to News Papers." It is through these writings that we know what happened during Grant's visit to St. Augustine. While these scrapbooks have provided a wealth of information, they have also provided a mystery as to the year when Grant visited. A clipping from the *Newark Daily Advertiser* is dated Saturday, January 17, 1879. This error has been repeated many times, but researcher Jessica A. May has conclusively proven the year to be 1880.[78]

The Grant party arrived via private rail car in St. Augustine on Wednesday, January 14, to much celebration. The president's party included Lieutenant General Philip Sheridan and his wife. Upon disembarking from the car, there was a rush of people: "One old colored woman appeared in her cart, draped in an old flag, with a large wreath of moss, evergreens and roses, around her horse's neck. When the General passed her, the old lady saluted him, and sang out at the top of her voice, 'Dat's you, God bless you!' the General returned the salute, which raised quite a laugh."

Philip Sheridan served as an infantry general in the western theater of the war before being brought to the east as a cavalry general under Ulysses S. Grant. He would later serve as general-in-chief of the army. *Courtesy Library of Congress.*

Colonel Albert Tracy and a welcoming committee of prominent citizens met Grant and introduced him to Mayor George Greeno, who provided a welcoming speech. President Grant gave a brief oration for those gathered at the depot:

> *I thank you for your kind welcome. I have seen something of your State, and am greatly pleased with it. Florida is the oldest settled State, but really the youngest in development. From what I have seen I am convinced that it will in time produce more than any other State, that is, from the soil. It cannot, of course, be expected to equal in manufactures and commerce many northern States. The soil products of some of our northwestern States was enormous, but I feel sure, although it may appear to be an exaggerated statement, that in time your sugar and semi-tropical fruits will exceed in value the products of any other State in the Union. Again I thank you for your kindly expressions of welcome.*[79]

The remarks over with, the parties loaded into at least sixteen carriages and left for the city and to take Generals Grant and Sheridan, along with their parties, to their accommodations at the St. Augustine Hotel, then located at the corner of the Plaza and Bayfront. The brief ride into town was eventful, as the road was full of those who had not made the journey to the train depot. Along the way, the entourage passed the St. Benedict Society, the Lincoln Temperance Society and more. Upon passing Senator Gilbert's home, they heard the St. Augustine cornet band. In front of Mr. Daniel's home was an arch made of evergreens and flowers with the words "Let us have peace." Stretching across King Street near the home of Dr. Anderson, a massive arch was awaiting the visitors with the welcome "Our oldest city greets our greatest General." Soldiers at the pier gave a twenty-one-gun salute in honor of Lieutenant General Sheridan.

That evening, the St. Augustine Hotel played host to an elegant party as officers and their wives from the St. Francis Barracks arrived to greet both Grant and Sheridan.

The following morning, a reception was held for the generals at Fort Marion. A room next to the chapel had been prepared, and it was here that the generals greeted a large number of locals: "Many of the colored people, neatly dressed and quiet in behavior, were delighted with the kindness which they found themselves received." Following the reception, the generals were given a tour of the fort by Sergeant McGuire. After an extensive tour, the families retired to the St. Francis Barracks, where they were entertained by

This artistic depiction of the welcome provided to Ulysses S. Grant while visiting Key West is similar to descriptions provided of Grant's visit to St. Augustine. *Courtesy State Archives of Florida.*

General and Mrs. Dent. Lunch included a bountiful supply of strawberries, which must have been a delicacy because they were singled out by Ammidown in his report. The afternoon ended with Grant and Sheridan visiting Dent at his home. There, the two Civil War veterans each planted an orange tree.

Thursday ended with a ball presented by W.W. Palmer and held at the Magnolia Hotel. The event was well attended by both young and old. Ammidown describes the scene, showing that no expense was spared in showing guests a good time:

> *The ball was one of the finest given to the General yet in the south. The ball-room was a tropical scene quite worthy of description, and highly creditable to the tastes of Mrs. W.W. Palmer, the charming wife of the proprietor, who arranged the decorations. On each side of the main entrance to the ball-room (converted from the dining hall) stood a large-sized banana plant, bearing a full bunch of bananas. Around each of the eight columns in the hall was entwined vines and mosses a different variety to each pillar, each trimmed at the top with heavy clusters of ripe oranges. Large clusters of*

> *magnolia branches, and palmettos were grouped in each corner under which were placed young alligators of three feet in length particularly hidden in Spanish mosses. Large banks of flowers each containing bushels of white, pink, and red roses were ranged along that sides, and hung in wreaths on the walls, and all had been gathered right from the gardens about town the same day. It was a glorious display for midwinter in the United States, and was warmly admired by all, especially the northern visitors present.*[30]

After all the excitement of the first two days in town, the generals were allowed a brief respite on Friday. Commodore Douglas and the St. Augustine

A view of the large Holmes Ammidown house. It was here that Ammidown entertained Ulysses and Julia Grant during their stay in St. Augustine. *Courtesy State Archives of Florida.*

Yacht Club arranged for the generals and their families to go on a fishing trip. Ammidown makes no mention of what, if anything, they caught.

Saturday was again a day of events and parties. At 5:00 p.m., the Ammidowns hosted an invitation-only reception at their St. George Street home. Not shy about self-promotion, Ammidown describes an event with fountains, flowers, music, good food and "everybody in a glee" all "under Heaven's open canopy."

There was one last party for the illustrious visitors. Captain E.E. Vaill presented a grand ball at the St. Augustine Hotel in honor of the Grant and Sheridan families. The event was well attended despite not getting started until about 8:00 p.m. The hotel orchestra kept guests dancing all night. The reporting of the event read like a who's who in St. Augustine, with names and descriptions of dress being given. Ammidown used this final event as a chance to talk with Julia Grant and said that "she would like St. Augustine for Winter residence if they had a cozy home, and spoke of one or two quiet places here that pleased her, etc. I think the lady would make a most pleasant and 'neighborly' neighbor."[81]

FRANKLIN W. SMITH

The name Franklin W. Smith is not one that will have meaning to many. However, he had a close association to both Abraham Lincoln and the city of St. Augustine. Smith and his bride of less than two weeks, Laura Beven, attended the March 4, 1861 Lincoln inaugural ball. At the time, it was said that Laura wore her wedding dress, and she was considered to be one of the seven most beautiful women present. *Frank Leslie's Illustrated Newspaper* had this to say: "Mrs. Frank Smith, of Boston, wore a dress the charm of which was its extreme and exquisite simplicity. It consisted of white watered satin skirt, robe and train. In style and taste it was the perfection of the modistes' art. The head-dress was both rich and recherché."[82]

Smith and his brother Benjamin were partners in a well-known and respected hardware firm that did contract business with the United States Navy. The Smith brothers were known for their integrity and detested seeing the government taken advantage of by dishonest contractors selling goods at prices well above what they should be. Franklin was vocal in calling out fraud, taking to self-publishing pamphlets that would list his charges and the names of those he considered guilty. This willingness to not participate in the questionable

Serving as secretary of the navy during the Civil War, Gideon Welles was instrumental in carrying out the Union blockade of Southern ports. Welles clashed with Abraham Lincoln, however, in regard to Franklin W. Smith. *Courtesy Library of Congress.*

activities of other contractors and government employees, plus the naming of those who were not honest, put the Smith brothers in a difficult position, and they found themselves under intense scrutiny.

On the morning of June 17, 1864, through an order from Secretary of the Navy Gideon Welles, Franklin Smith was physically taken from his home, placed on a boat and taken to Fort Warren on Georges Island. That afternoon, his brother met the same fate. Their homes and business were raided, files and desks ransacked and safes broken into and contents removed, all without the benefit of a warrant.

Smith was held for two weeks before bail arrangements could be agreed upon. The crime the brothers were finally accused of was "fraud upon the United States." His trial was scheduled to take place in Philadelphia, far from family, witnesses and his defense counsel. In addition, the trial was not to be in federal court but rather was to be a naval court-martial. Upon hearing this, the senators from Massachusetts complained to Secretary Welles, but he would not intervene. The senators then took their case to Lincoln, who ordered the court-martial moved to Boston.

During the four-month trial, the prosecution claimed that Smith had provided an inferior type of tin, lower-quality hardware, machine-made files rather than handmade ones and secondhand anchors rather than new ones. Smith was able to refute many of these charges, with the navy being unable to prove certain items were from the Smith company. The question of different types of tin was explained away by Smith. While, yes, they had supplied the cheaper revely tin and not the banca tin called for, they had only billed the

Senator Charles Sumner was instrumental in obtaining presidential support for Franklin W. Smith. Reproduction of a painting by Edgar Parker. *Courtesy Library of Congress.*

government for the cheaper material. With supplies being tight, this type of arrangement was commonplace. To call this fraud was pushing the definition of the word. Despite the overall flimsiness of the charges, the expected guilty verdict was reached.

It was then that Senator Charles Sumner really took up the cause of Franklin Smith. On March 17, 1865, he met with President Lincoln, riding in a carriage with Lincoln and his wife and pleading his case that Smith was innocent and that the charges were in retaliation for his earlier claims of fraud. Lincoln finally agreed to meet with Sumner again after his daily engagements were done and discuss the case further. The two met that evening from 10:00 p.m. until after midnight. Lincoln made his decision and put it in writing for Sumner to pick up that morning:

> *I am unwilling for the sentence to stand, and be executed, to any extent, in this case. In the absence of a more adequate motive than the evidence discloses, I am wholly unable to believe in the existence of criminal or fraudulent intent on the part of one of such well-established good character, as is the accused. If the evidence went so far to establish a guilty profit of one or two hundred thousand dollars, as it does of one or two hundred dollars, this case would, on the question of guilt, bear a far different aspect. That on this contract, involving from one million to twelve hundred thousand dollars, the contractors should attempt a fraud which at the most could profit them only one or two hundred, or even one thousand dollars, is to my mind beyond the power of rational belief. That they did not, in such a case, strike for greater gains proves that they did not, with guilty or fraudulent intent, strike at all. Judgment and*

sentence are disapproved, and declared null, and the accused ordered to be discharged.[83]

In April 1865, Smith was selected to lead the gathering at the Tremont Temple in Boston after the assassination of Abraham Lincoln. The Tremont

The Tremont Temple in Boston is home to a Baptist congregation that traces its roots to the 1840s. The building has often been used for public events and in prewar days was often used for antislavery speeches. *Courtesy Library of Congress.*

Temple has other Lincoln associations as well. At one time, the building that housed the church had been a theater. That theater was managed by Junius Brutus Booth, the father of John Wilkes Booth, Lincoln's assassin. Later, in 1848, while in Boston stumping for Zachary Taylor, Lincoln shared billing with his future secretary of state, William Seward. Seward gave an antislavery speech that moved Lincoln to have allegedly said, "I have been thinking about what you said in your speech. I reckon you are right. We have got to deal with this slavery question, and got to give more attention to it hereafter than we have been doing."[84]

Named for one of the princesses in Washington Irving's book *The Alhambra*, Franklin W. Smith's Moorish-inspired masterpiece, Villa Zorayda, is now a museum. *Courtesy State Archives of Florida.*

Smith was now a free but somewhat embittered man: "In 1865 my capital was greatly reduced as a result of the historical case of the United States against Franklin W. Smith; (with a final vindication by President Lincoln, stated by Senator Charles Sumner in his works, as probably the last of his actions of such a character). It cost me Forty Thousand Dollars in defense. Impaired health compelled my retirement from my profitable business and the luxurious life on Beacon Street was abandoned."[85]

Smith's in-laws built a home in St. Augustine, and it was during a visit to see them that he decided he would like to have a home there as well. In late 1883, he and a builder from Boston began experimenting with the local coquina, mixing it with the new product Portland cement. Using their new mixture, the concrete was poured into molds that were ten inches tall. Once this mixture had set, the forms were raised and a new level poured. This continued until the building was complete. To ensure stability, railroad ties were run through the walls.

Henry Flagler, along with John D. Rockefeller and others, was a founder of the Standard Oil Company. Later in life, Flagler turned his attention to Florida and was instrumental in developing the state as a tourist destination. He built numerous buildings in St. Augustine, and Flagler College bears his name. *Courtesy State Archives of Florida.*

Named Villa Zorayda after the second princess in Washington Irving's *The Alhambra*, the home caught the eye of wealthy investor Henry Flagler of Standard Oil fame. Flagler attempted to purchase Villa Zorayda as a gift for his new bride, Ida. Smith declined the offer but did show Flagler the benefits of his poured concrete technique. Flagler would use this technique when he later built the Hotel Ponce de Leon (now part of Flagler College), the Alcazar (now government offices, a museum and retail space), the Memorial Presbyterian Church and the Grace Methodist Church.[86]

Smith himself became a St. Augustine hotel owner, if only for a short period of time. On land purchased from Henry Flagler, Smith built the Casa Monica

Built with his preferred poured concrete method, the Casa Monica Hotel was owned by Franklin W. Smith before financial difficulties led to his selling the property to Henry Flagler. From the 1960s until the late 1990s, the building was used for governmental offices before being returned to its original purpose as a hotel. *Courtesy State Archives of Florida.*

Hotel in 1887. Built with the poured concrete technique, the hotel features numerous architectural details. Despite its beauty, however, the hotel was a financial drain, and Smith ended up selling the property to Flagler after the winter season ended. The sales price was $325,000.[37]

Smith and his wife separated in the 1890s, and his financial health continued to decline. In 1906, his St. Augustine property, among others, was foreclosed upon, and Smith ultimately returned to Boston, where he died in 1911.

LINCOLNVILLE HISTORIC DISTRICT

The Lincolnville Historic District is an area of St. Augustine that was founded by freed slaves around 1866. The area encompasses approximately 140 acres, or about fifty blocks. The district is bounded by Cedar, Riviera, Cerra, Washington and DeSoto Streets. Lincolnville contains the largest assortment of Victorian-era homes in St. Augustine and in 1991 was added to the National Register of Historic Places.

The elections of 1869 were the first in which African American men were allowed to vote. During the Reconstruction period, the Lincolnville

Charles "Bossy" Benet served as marshal in St. Johns County. On October 31, 1902, he shot and wounded Alderman John Papino. Despite witnesses and admitting to the shooting, Benet was never convicted. *Courtesy State Archives of Florida.*

area produced local leaders including Domingo M. Pappy. Pappy served as a St. Johns County commissioner from 1873 to 1875, St. Johns County tax assessor from 1876 to 1877, St. Augustine councilman from 1877 to 1878 and 1884 to 1886 and also as St. Augustine tax assessor from 1880 to 1881. The post-Reconstruction era in St. Augustine was similar to that in many other southern cities, with strict voter requirements and voter intimidation. During the 1880s, the town was divided into political wards, with black families generally being clustered into a single ward. This geographic isolation helped lessen their political reach, and in 1902, John Papino, the last black elected to office until 1973, was shot by Marshal Charles Benet during a city council meeting. The shooter claimed Papino would not be quiet while he was trying to address the entire council. Papino survived his wounds, but Benet was never convicted of a crime.[88]

The post-Reconstruction segregation led to a growing business district in the Lincolnville area. While it is true that many blacks of the time were farmers or worked in domestic jobs, there was a growing class of ministers, barbers, shoemakers and repairmen, bankers and other skilled labor jobs. Businesses such as the Lincoln Theatre, located at 92 Washington Street, filled the demand for services in the area, as is shown in a local newspaper article: "Crowded to the walls the Lincoln Motion Picture Theatre opened Saturday night and enjoyed a business that was limited to the capacity of the house. The great opening success augurs well for the future."[89]

Chapter 5

African Americans

The story of African Americans in St. Augustine during the Civil War era is one of hope mixed with success and failure. Leading up to the war, slavery was common. Yet there were a number of freemen, though the percentage was not high. During the war, freedom came to those in bonds earlier than in many areas due to the Union occupation of the city. After the war, there was a concerted effort on the part of the Catholic Church to educate those newly freed, particularly the children, despite the political difficulties faced by black citizens.

The United States Census of 1850 shows that the total population of St. Johns County was just over 2,500. Of this number, 1,400 were white, with roughly 1,000 being slaves and about 100 freemen; around 40 percent of the population was enslaved. In the city of St. Augustine proper, the percentage of slaves to the total population was slightly lower, with a total population of 1,934. Whites accounted for 1,213, with the number of slaves being 631. Free blacks numbered only 90. The slave percentage in St. Augustine in 1850 was just under 33 percent.

By 1860, however, the population of St. Johns County had increased to slightly over 3,000, but the number of slaves had not increased and stayed at roughly 1,000, or a drop to 33 percent. The number of free blacks decreased to around 80. Population changes were more dramatic for the city of St. Augustine, with the total population dipping slightly to 1,914. Whites accounted for 1,175, free blacks numbered 67 and slaves totaled 672, or an increase to 35 percent.

St. Johns County was primarily a rural area in this time frame, with family farming being of vital importance. Agricultural records from the period show increases in almost every category from 1850 through 1860. By 1860, improved farmland in the county was valued at nearly $70,000, and there was over $6,000 worth of farm machinery in use. The year 1860 saw approximately eleven thousand bushels of Indian corn, over fifteen thousand bushels of potatoes, nearly 5,500 pounds of butter, 9,000 pounds of rice, 30,000 pounds of cane sugar and over 4,500 gallons of molasses produced. Despite any advances in technology, production like this was still heavily dependent on the forced labor of slaves.

Census records from 1860 show that 136 persons owned slaves in St. Johns County, meaning the average slaveholder owned just over 7 slaves. In 1860, St. Johns County had 1,953 white citizens, and 7 percent of the population owned slaves. By 1860, wealth appears to have been consolidating as well, with 27, or approximately 20 percent, of slaveholding individuals owning 10 or more slaves.

This compares to 1850, when 131 persons owned slaves and the average slaveholder held just over 7.5 slaves. The white population of St. Johns County at the time was 1,417, which equates to slightly over 9 percent being slaveholders. In 1850, there were only 16, or 12 percent of slaveholders, owning 10 or more slaves. These mixed numbers show that slavery was not expanding in St. Johns County but had perhaps begun the inevitable decline many had predicted.

Despite living in an era when women were seldom able to hold property, there were over thirty women in the county shown as owning slaves on the Slave Schedule of 1860. The woman with the largest ownership of slaves was Elizabeth DuPont, who owned thirty-one slaves. Another large slaveholder was Catherine Solano, who in 1860 owned twenty-nine slaves. The federal census shows her age as seventy with $5,000 worth of real estate and personal property worth $15,000. In 1850, she was known as Catalina Solano and owned twenty-four slaves and had real estate holdings of $4,000.

The largest slave owner in St. Johns County in the immediate prewar period of 1860 was Venancio Sanchez. Sanchez was born in 1809 to parents Jose and Christina (Hill) Sanchez of St. Augustine during the Second Spanish Period and served as a second lieutenant in the Second Florida Mounted Militia during the Florida Indian Wars of 1835–38. After the Indian Wars, he married Carlotta (possibly Charlotta) Perpall in 1846. Venancio and Carlotta had two children, son William and daughter Jessie, and it appears that Carlotta passed away before 1860. Venancio was a merchant, selling both dry goods and groceries. He operated his business on busy King Street across from the Plaza in the area between Aviles Street and the Trinity Episcopal Church. For several years, members of the Perpall family served as clerks in the store.

By 1850, Venancio and Carlotta were well on their way to being considered wealthy. Venancio is listed as the owner of twenty slaves, and his real estate is listed as valued at $8,000. Despite having lost his wife, by 1860, Sanchez owned seventy-four slaves. His real estate holdings were now listed as worth only $5,839, but he had personal property valued at $6,370. Although he lost his slave property and dealt with the other issues associated with the war, by 1870, Sanchez could still boast real estate worth $10,000 and personal property valued at $5,000. His young son William was in the family business now as well.[90] Despite his apparent wealth, there was anger in Venancio over the war and its outcome:

> *Times are very hard in this quarter, the privileges of being a Southern man at this time are very small, no one but a carpetbagger or a Scalawag, or an African who are said by all honest men to be void of principle or honesty can hold or keep possession of all lucrative offices. Although we have not had to take the oath of allegiance, yet we are not allowed to sit or act as jurors, but the meanest negro has the right to act as juror & to hold office. We have not as yet succeeded in getting possession of any of our property & the truth is that I can see no chance of being able to succeed as long as the radical party has the right of government in their hands as they have all things their own way, right or wrong...I am heartily disgusted with this so-called Glorious Union & feel that I would prefer to live under the flag of any other nation...Time may bring about a chance for the better.*[91]

Records show that Venancio possibly fathered a son with a slave named Julia around the time of the death of his wife. According to Freedman's Bank Records, Robert Sanchez was the son of Venancio and Julia Sanchez. His birth year can be calculated to about 1855. Little mention is ever made of Robert, and he does not show up on census records until 1880, when he is listed as a mulatto now living in Oak Hill, Florida, with his wife, Louisa, two sons and a boarder. By 1885, the family had grown to include another son and a daughter. By 1910, Robert was a widower with a family to support, so he and his family had moved north to Rhode Island, where the men worked as fishermen. In 1920, Robert was still working as a fisherman and was living with only a boarder in his home. Robert's January 1926 obituary gives another clue that he was related to the Venancio Sanchez family. His surviving relatives list a brother, William, who lived in St. Augustine. William Sanchez, the son of Venancio, did not die until September 1927.[92]

THE SLAVE MARKET

Little is known about the overall slave trade in St. Augustine. Despite being a port city, it appears that St. Augustine was not a major area where slaves were imported and sold prior to the banning of the slave trade in 1808. This could partly be due to the dangerous conditions offshore and the associated difficulty of getting a ship to harbor but is most likely due to the lack of population and wealth in the area. Despite not being able to import slaves, the internal slave trade continued to grow and was a source of wealth for many. Florida, with a comparatively small population and overall lack of assets, does not appear to have widely participated in comparison to its cotton-producing sister states.

When one thinks of slave markets, the mind is immediately drawn to cities such as New Orleans and Charleston. These cities were known for their large public auctions where men, women and children were herded like cattle, stuffed in holding pens and then paraded before potential bidders. In many instances, families were broken apart with little to no concern for the welfare of children or the sanctity of marriage. Those slaves who were young, well behaved and of good health often brought the most money. While having a skill could be important, most buyers were looking for field hands who could bring in more revenue than it cost to maintain them.

Located in the Plaza is an open-air building known by the name Public Market or sometimes by the fancifully titled Slave Market. There is little evidence showing that the building was a slave market in the sense that we think of that term today. The moniker "Slave Market" appears to have come into being after the Civil War. Perhaps the earliest printed record comes from regional promoter Max Bloomfield:

> *East of the Confederate monument stands the old, old market. A queer-looking structure it is. 'Tis hard to name its style of architecture, therefore we will call it a piece of Augustinian mechanism. Four years ago it was used as a meat market, but since, the Council and a private gentleman have rescued it from what must have been degrading to this proud piece of*

> *Spanish antiquity, of which very little is known. We have been told that before the war it was used as a slave market. Whenever a sale was to take place the bell in the cupola would be rung to notify the public. The reader will please understand that the compiler of this Guide does not hold himself responsible for the slave-market story, but, in the words of the old sergeant at the fort, will say: "I'm only giving it to ye as it was given to me, d'ye moind now?"*[93]

From the same period, the English author Lady Mary Anne Duffus Hardy wrote of her travels in the South:

> *There is the "Plaza de la Constitution," where the good Christians burnt their bretheren a century ago; it is a large square, laid out with grass plots, and flower beds, with paths cut through, leading from one side of the Plaza to the other. In the centre stands the curious old market-place, roofed in at the top, but open on all sides; this was the ancient slave mart, where "God's image carved in ebony," was bought and sold in most ungodly fashion; there is the place where they stood, ranged in rows like cattle in a pen, so that their purchasers might walk to and fro examining them from all points to see that they had their money's worth. They sit there now, these self same slaves of the old days, with bright kerchiefs round their heads, surrounded by fruits and flowers, buying and selling on their own account, laughing, chaffing, bargaining with one another with the easy air that freedom gives.*[94]

To the modern reader, both of these seem to really be just flights of fancy rather than any kind of accurate historical documentation. In fact, neither writer references where they heard these stories, so both should be taken with a grain of salt.

Union soldiers who were quartered in the city held differing views as to the market as well. The regimental historian of the Forty-eighth New York believed the structure to have been a slave market: "I looked across square, past the old building with the open front, formerly used as a slave market, to the office of the commissary." A diarist from the Fourth New Hampshire, however, fails to mention such a use of the market: "This faced the square, an open green space, which we passed in marching up from the wharf. Here was also a market, to which was brought every day the produce of the market-gardens about the city."[95]

Perhaps, however, the individual who played the largest role in creating the "slave market" name and image was St. Augustine photographer W.J.

This postcard helped to perpetuate and promote the myth of the Slave Market in St. Augustine. *Courtesy the author.*

Harris. Harris, who also for a time served as the business manager for the St. Augustine Historical Society, created a postcard that on the front featured an elderly black man with a basket over his right arm using a cane in his left hand to steady himself. One the back it is labeled: "OLD SLAVE MARKET ST. AUGUSTINE, FLA. The Old Slave Market in the east end of the Plaza is an interesting landmark of antebellum days. Old slave in foreground." The card sold well to tourists, as might be expected, and copies were sent all over the country, but the ensuing controversy over the claim led Harris to issue a revised version of the card. While the front stayed the same, the back of the card now said: "OLD SLAVE MARKET ST. AUGUSTINE, FLA. The old slave market in the east end of the Plaza is an interesting landmark of antebellum days. Built in 1840 for a public market. Called 'slave market' by an enterprising photographer to make his picture sell."

In opposition to Harris stands Mr. J. Gardner, who in 1914 wrote:

> *Since the close of the war I have seen the pictures with the legend "The Old Slave Market." I want to state that this is a fabrication, to pander to the morbid tastes of a certain class that come or came down to our section with the hope and desire to see only the revolting or objectionable side of the picture. This market when I knew it stood near the Plaza, if my memory*

> *serves me, and only fish, meat vegetables, etc., were sold, but I never heard of a "nigger" being sold there.*[96]

Mr. Gardner claimed to have been about seventeen years old at the time of the war, but it should also be noted that when writing this, he was doing so for the St. Augustine Historical Society and Institute of Science.

While the market is not known to have been widely used as an area for slave sales, there is evidence that the sale of slaves did take place there. Local historian David Nolan has done research showing that on several occasions there is documentary proof of slave sales having taken place in the market area. An 1834 advertisement for an estate sale happening "at the market House in the City of St. Augustine" would include "a very prime gang of 30 negroes, accustomed to the culture of Sugar and Cotton." Notice was given in 1836 that "two slaves with their increase if any are to be sold at Public Auction to the highest bidder at the Market House." In 1838, a "negro woman Sally" was sold out of the estate of Mary Hanford "at the Market House." This is certainly not a large number but does lead one to believe that other sales could have taken place there.[97]

While in St. Augustine seeking a cure for tuberculosis, Ralph Waldo Emerson heard a slave auction taking place near the Government House. *Courtesy Library of Congress.*

In addition to these limited instances, the philosopher and poet Ralph Waldo Emerson made note of a slave auction that took place in the general area of the market. Emerson spent more than two months in St. Augustine during 1827 due to consumption, or tuberculosis as we know it, a disease that had already killed his father and a brother. The warm temperatures and soothing sea air were considered the best remedies at the time. Being a northerner, his trip south was his first true look at slavery. While in St. Augustine, he wrote:

> *A fortnight since I attended a meeting of the Bible Society. The treasurer of this institution is Marshall of the district & by a somewhat unfortunate arrangement had appointed a special meeting of the Society & a slave auction at the same time & place, one being in Government house & the other in the adjoining yard. One ear therefore heard the glad tidings of great joy whilst the other was regaled with "going gentlemen, going!" And almost without changing our position we might aid in sending the scriptures to Africa or bid for "four children without the mother" who had been kidnapped therefrom.*[98]

Florida politician David Levy Yulee spent $7,180 at a St. Augustine slave auction in November 1845. His purchase included twenty-four men, women and children ranging in age from two through seventy-five. Yulee's wife, Nannie, in September 1849 purchased from Bartolo Oliveros "a certain negro slave belonging to me named Henry." Neither record details an exact location as to the place of sale in St. Augustine, but it would certainly have made sense for the auction that Mr. Yulee participated in to have taken place at a central location such as the Plaza.[99]

The first Jewish member of the United States Senate, David Levy Yulee also served in the Confederate Congress as a delegate from Florida. Yulee spent much of his professional life in the railroad industry and also owned a large sugar cane plantation that was farmed with slave labor. *Courtesy Library of Congress.*

The market still stands today and is still used. Local artists can often be seen selling their wares to tourists and locals alike. The many trams and horse-drawn carriages that pass by daily will still make reference to the "slave market," helping to perpetuate the story. The informational plaque attached to the market structure also feeds into the slave market story: "From 1605 to 1765 there stood on this site a guard house and watch tower.

Under British rule it became the market and place of public auction ever since called the slave market."

EMANCIPATION

Fresh from Union victory at the Battle of Antietam, Abraham Lincoln was emboldened to issue his Emancipation Proclamation. This turned the war into a battle to free slaves and not just to bring the Confederate states back into the Union. On January 1, 1863, the proclamation took effect. In many ways, this only gave lip service to freeing slaves, as slaves in states not in rebellion were not freed. Also, Confederate states did not recognize Lincoln's authority over them, so only in areas controlled by Union troops did the proclamation take effect.

While it is impossible to determine the number of slaves who were actually freed in early January 1863, St. Augustine was one of these areas in which the Emancipation Proclamation was enforced. The announcement was difficult for slaveholders, as was recounted by a soldier: "With the owners of the slaves, this announcement of freedom created the greatest excitement, for they felt its consequences. They had subsisted upon the earning of the slaves, and it was a serious matter to them that their riches should take legs and run away."[100] The soldier's words are backed up by a letter from former St. Augustine merchant Christian Boye to his son after the loss of fifteen slaves:

> *Those slaves of mine were worth to me a year ago seventeen thousand dollars and there was some 10 young ones among them who increased in value every day. My yearly income from them was not less than $2000.00 to $2500.00. I could afford to send you and your sister to expensive schools…This income is stopped, and God knows when it will begin again. I am obliged to use strictest economy, turn a penny a dozen times before I spend it. The loss of our slaves forces me to take Mary from school…as I cannot make enough to pay her school bills.*[101]

The most vivid account of slaves being freed comes from a 1934 telling by Mary Ann Murray. The then-eighty-five-year-old recounted that "word of the Emancipation Proclamation reached here and, she said, all the slaveholders were ordered to release their slaves and allow them to gather in a large vacant lot west of St. Joseph's Academy, where they were officially freed." This site, while now partly used as a parking lot, is oftentimes called "Liberation Lot."[102]

For decades afterward, Emancipation Day was celebrated in earnest by the black citizens of St. Augustine. A historian of the Twenty-fourth Massachusetts recalled the event being celebrated as early as 1864:

> *New Year's Day in St. Augustine was an institution. To begin with it was the first anniversary of the Emancipation Proclamation or its application, and the colored population made the most of it; nor was the celebration confined to them, since the regimental bands played the old year out and the new one in. A stage or platform had been erected on the plaza for the speakers and, at 11 a.m., the colored people, several hundred in number, came marching up to the stage by twos, old and young, and of both sexes. Union officers and men were also present and, first in order, was the reading of the famous proclamation; the bands played, Judge Stickney presided, Chaplains Trumbull and Wilson spoke, and the colored preachers told the people what was expected of them.*[103]

A car decorated for the Lincolnville parade. Original photograph by Richard A. Twine. *Courtesy State Archives of Florida.*

As the years progressed, one of the highlights of the celebration was the parade, which, according to David Nolan, began at St. Benedict School and made its way up Washington Street, around the Plaza and down to Lewis Park near the old Flagler Hospital.

BLACK CONFEDERATES

The claim that there were large numbers of blacks who fought for the Confederacy continues to be put forth. The statistics from St. Augustine and St. Johns County do not back up these claims. Only 3 out of nearly 1,100 black citizens from St. Johns County are known to have been associated with the Confederate army. The three men were all listed as being members of the Third Florida Company B or, as they were commonly called, the St. Augustine Blues.

The first soldier has a bit of mystery as to his name. The man who is listed as having served in the Confederate army is Tony Fontane. Fontane was born in either 1810 or 1813 and enlisted in May 1861 as a musician. He was discharged from service in November 1862 for being overage. There is no known record of him participating in battle. In 1880, he was still using the name Fontane, but by 1885 in the Florida State Census, he used the name Antonio Welters, which is the same name used in the 1900 Federal Census. Fontane/Welters died in 1902. He is buried in San Lorenzo Cemetery under a Confederate marker with the name Anthony T. Welters carved on it. When his wife, Cedra (sometimes spelled Sedra), applied to the State of Florida for a widow's pension in 1909, she listed her husband's name as Tony Fontane. To prove just how divisive the war could be, Tony had a young son John who served in the Thirty-third United States Colored Infantry as a musician. The younger Welters is also buried in San Lorenzo Cemetery but under a Union headstone. According to stories told after the war, Welters was considered to be a "highly respected colored citizen." The Welters family continued to leave its mark on St. Augustine, with descendants holding jobs such as restaurant owner, teacher and dentist.

Emanuel Osborne, born in 1843, was said to be the son of freed slaves. In May 1861, he enlisted in the St. Augustine Blues as a private and was, according to his pension application, discharged in November 1862 at the end of his enlistment period. After the war, Osborne, who was unable to read or write, held a variety of jobs such as seaman, laborer and church sexton. His first wife, Elizabeth, passed away sometime before 1879, and he then married Mary Anne Lang. Lang, who was several years older, brought five children to the marriage, and she and Emanuel had at least two more. By 1900, the family was living on Washington Street next door to the Welters family. Emanuel passed away in April 1907 and is buried in San Lorenzo Cemetery under a Confederate headstone.

Little is known about the life of Isaac Papino. He was born in 1813 and was enlisted by Captain John Lott Phillips on May 24, 1861, serving as a musician. He was discharged from service in November 1862. A Confederate marker stands in San Lorenzo Cemetery in honor of Musician Papino.[101]

Alexander H. Darnes

While relatively little is known about him, Alexander Darnes is one of the great former slave stories from the postwar era. Darnes was born into slavery, the son of Violent Pinkey. Violent was owned by the family of future Confederate lieutenant general Edmund Kirby Smith. The story is told that he was born in the same home as Edmund.

In 1855, Darnes was sent to serve then Captain Edmund Kirby Smith while he served in the western territories. With the outbreak of the Civil War and Smith pledging his allegiance to the Confederacy, Darnes followed along, continuing to serve Smith. No mention is ever made of Darnes being considered a Confederate soldier.

After the conclusion of the war and having been freed, Darnes attended Lincoln University and in 1880 received a medical degree from Howard University. He was to become only the second black doctor in Florida and the first in Jacksonville when he opened his practice. An 1884 *New York Globe* article commented on the success Darnes was having by reporting that he lived in a large home in an upper-class neighborhood on Ocean Street.

Darnes's success was not only monetary, as was shown by James Weldon Johnson. Johnson looked up to Darnes and told of the two being friends while Johnson was young: "Dr. Darnes made himself a bug chum to Rosamond and me, and we liked him tremendously. He consistently brought us some of the odd and ends so much prized by boys. He once gave us fifty cents apiece for learning the deaf and dumb alphabet within a given time…But best of all, Dr. Darnes was an enthusiastic fisherman who opened up a new world of fun and sport by teaching us how to fish."[105]

Darnes passed away on February 11, 1894, and was commemorated in an obituary stating:

> *The largest number of people ever gathered within the walls of any church in this city was at Mt. Zion A.M.E. Church yesterday to attend the funeral of Dr. A.H. Darnes deceased. Long before the appointed time for the ceremonies to begin, people could be seen coming from every direction winding their way towards the church, and by 1 o'clock p.m. the church was already crowded...Dr. Darnes, the deceased, was about 48 years of age, and had been a popular practicing physician in this city for about 16 years, and rendered valuable services during the smallpox and yellow fever epidemics.*[106]

He was buried in Old City Cemetery in Jacksonville.

On November 8, 2004, a statue memorializing Dr. Alexander H. Darnes and Professor/General Edmund Kirby Smith was unveiled in the garden of what is now the St. Augustine Historical Society Research Library. The library building is the former home of Darnes and Smith. The life-size bronze sculpture, commonly called *The Sons of St. Augustine*, is the work of Maria Kirby-Smith, the great-granddaughter of the general. The statue features Darnes as a doctor with his medical bag on the ground between the men. His association with the Freemasons is also shown in the detail work on his watch fob. Smith is portrayed in his academic regalia. Smith had served as president at the University of Nashville and later was a professor of mathematics at the University of the South.[107]

Chapter 6

Civil War Generals in St. Augustine

St. Augustine was long used as a military outpost due to its location and the presence of Fort Marion. As such, many generals, both Union and Confederate, went through the town, some leaving a bigger mark than others. Several were born in the city, some died there and some just happened to live part of their lives there.

Stephen Vincent Benet

Stephen Vincent Benet is most commonly known for being the grandfather of the author by the same name who famously penned "John Brown's Body." Benet did not serve as a general during the Civil War; however, he was promoted to this rank afterward.

Benet was born in St. Augustine on January 22, 1827, the second child to Pedro (sometimes referred to as Peter) Benet and Juana Hernandez. According to an obituary, he was born in a house on the corner of St. George and Cuna Streets. The Benet family was of Minorcan descent, and Pedro was a highly respected member of the small community. As a public servant, he served in various roles, including police officer, justice of the peace and surveyor of the port. He also appears to have been well off and is shown as owning fourteen slaves on the 1860 Federal Census. This wealth allowed Pedro to send young Stephen to private schools. Pedro was

Because of his wealth and political influence, Pedro Benet was nicknamed "King of the Minorcans." *Courtesy State Archives of Florida.*

so highly thought of that he was given the nickname "King of the Minorcans."

At age twelve, Stephen was sent to Hallowell's School in Alexandria, Virginia. Around age sixteen, he was admitted to the University of Georgia, where he was to study only briefly. While in Athens, Georgia, he was appointed to the United States Military Academy at West Point. In 1849, Benet became the first graduate at West Point from the state of Florida, graduating third in a class of forty-three. It was then that Benet embarked on a long military career, being assigned to the Ordnance Corps.

Benet served in several different arsenals until receiving command in 1853 of the Pikesville Arsenal in Maryland. He then served in several different capacities until being appointed the principal assistant professor of geography, history and ethics at the U.S. Military Academy from 1859 to 1861. In 1861, he was appointed instructor of ordnance and the science of gunnery at the academy. He served in this role

Stephen Vincent Benet was the grandfather of the famous poet with the same name. *Courtesy Library of Congress.*

until 1864, when he again served as a commander, only this time at Frankford Arsenal in Philadelphia.

By 1869, Benet had been promoted to assistant to the chief of ordnance and in 1874 was promoted to chief of ordnance with the rank of brigadier general. He served in this position from June 1874 until his retirement in January 1891.

Throughout his life, Benet continued to be an academic. He published a translation of Jomini's *Political and Military History of the Battle of Waterloo* in 1853 and was the author of *A Treatise on Military Law and the Practice of Court Martials* in 1862 and also *Electro-ballistic Machines and the Schultz' Chronoscope* in 1866. According to the June 26, 1884 *Evening Star* newspaper, out of Washington, D.C., General Benet was awarded a doctor of law degree from Georgetown University on that day.

Brigadier General Stephen Vincent Benet passed away on his birthday in 1895 at the age of sixty-eight. He is buried in Arlington National Cemetery.[108]

EDMUND JACKSON DAVIS

Edmund J. Davis was born in St. Augustine on October 2, 1827, and spent his youth in the city. In 1848, he and his family moved to Galveston, Texas, where the young Davis studied law. He served as a customs inspector in Laredo, Texas, from 1850 to 1853, district attorney from 1853 to 1856 and then as a district

Born in St. Augustine, Edmund Davis served as a Union general during the war but spent much of his life in Texas, serving as governor from 1870 to 1874. *Courtesy Texas State Preservation Board.*

judge from 1856 to 1861. In 1861, Davis ran for election to serve in the Texas secession convention. Being an anti-secessionist, he was soundly defeated.

Not wanting to be subject to conscription in the Confederate army, Davis left the state, heading south into Mexico, where he raised the First Texas Cavalry (U.S.) from the large numbers of displaced Unionists in the country. Davis was appointed the regimental colonel. The First Texas Cavalry spent the war in the western theater, as might be expected. It started out serving in the defense of New Orleans, staying there until September 1863. For the next year, it moved around the areas of Louisiana, Texas and Mississippi. While seeing little fighting, the men did participate in the skirmish at Palmetto Ranch near the Mexican border in September 1864. Davis was not promoted to brigadier general until November 10, 1864, and was mustered out of service in August 1865.

After the war, Davis served as a delegate to the 1866 Texas constitutional convention and was its president in 1869. He would certainly have been called a radical, as he advocated an unrestricted right for Negro suffrage and the complete disfranchisement for all former Confederates and supporters, and he also wished to divide Texas into three states.

Union general Andrew Jackson Hamilton was defeated in the race for governor of Texas in 1869 by Edmund Davis. *Courtesy Texas State Preservation Board.*

In 1869, Davis was elected governor of Texas in what could at best be called a fixed election. Davis was the candidate being backed by the military, and because of this, it did almost everything in its power to ensure his election over the Democratic candidate, Andrew Jackson Hamilton. Hamilton, like Davis, had served as a Union general during the war; however, he had views much more conservative than those of Davis.

During the 1869 election, the military had voter registration lists redrawn and effectively eliminated much of the support Hamilton had. Many polling locations were not opened, and those that were open were manned by federal troops. Less than half the eligible white voters participated in the election. Despite these irregularities, Davis was only able to win the election by fewer than eight hundred votes. The new state constitution gave Davis wide powers and the ability to appoint over eight thousand state and local employees. With such power, Davis made plenty of friends and even more enemies. With the return to power of the Democratic Party in 1872, Davis's time in office was to be limited. His reelection campaign in 1873 turned into disaster, and he lost the election to Richard Coke by a two-to-one margin. Even though he was not to leave office until April 1874, he was forced out of office in January. His political career was pretty well over at this point; he later lost the 1880 election for governor and again lost in an 1882 bid for a congressional seat.

Davis passed away on February 7, 1883, in Austin, Texas, and is buried in State Cemetery.[109]

WILLIAM J. HARDEE

William Joseph Hardee was born on October 12, 1815, in Camden County, Georgia. He was the youngest child of Sarah Ellis and Major John Hardee. He was educated by a private tutor and was eventually granted entrance into the United States Military Academy at West

Confederate general William J. Hardee married into the prominent Dummett family and later owned the home that now serves as the St. Francis Inn. Anna Dummett helped to raise Hardee's children after her sister's death. *Courtesy Library of Congress.*

Point. He graduated twenty-sixth in a class of forty-five. Upon graduation, he was assigned to the Second U.S. Dragoons with the rank of second lieutenant in November 1838.

Soon after being assigned to the dragoons, Hardee was sent to Florida to help fight the Seminole Indians. He took sick in May 1840 and was sent to St. Augustine from June through October due to his illness. It was here that he met and married Elizabeth Dummett.

Elizabeth was the daughter of Mary and Thomas Dummett. It is Elizabeth and her sister Anna who figure into William Hardee's connection with St. Augustine. The Dummett girls were born in Barbados, and the family moved to Florida in 1825. Thomas purchased two plots of land, the first near the Tomoka River and the second near the Mosquito River, now called the Indian River. It was on these plots that Dummett grew sugar cane. A raid by Seminole Indians in 1835 chased the Dummett family north to St. Augustine. At that time, Thomas purchased the home on the corner of St. George and St. Francis Streets. This home has in some instances been incorrectly called the "governor's palace." It currently serves as the St. Francis Inn.[110]

It can safely be assumed that William Hardee and Elizabeth Dummett met during Hardee's time in St. Augustine in 1840. Hardee was returned to his regiment at Picolata in October 1840, and in November, he received orders sending him to France in order to study at the Royal Cavalry School in Saumur. Hardee and Dummett acted quickly, and on November 16, 1840, they were married by the Reverend R.H. Rutledge. As Hardee is alleged to have told his children, he "could not leave his beautiful sweetheart until she became his wife." The young couple was reunited in June 1842 at Hardee's new post in Louisiana.

Their reunion would be short-lived, however, as Elizabeth passed away in 1853 after contracting tuberculosis. The marriage had produced three daughters and a son who now relied on William for everything. William was able to rely on his unmarried sister-in-law Anna to take care of the children while he continued his military assignments. The Hardee children were not alone, as Anna was also the caregiver for the children of her sisters Mary and Sarah. In all, ten children lived in the home at the corner of St. George and St. Francis Streets.

In 1856, Hardee was made commandant at the U.S. Military Academy. It was through his position here that he came into contact with future Confederate States president Jefferson Davis. Davis was at that time serving as secretary of war and was changing the job of commandant to suit his own vision. In July 1856, Davis issued orders not just giving the commandant disciplinary control but also consolidating all tactical branches of instruction under his control as well.

During the summer of 1857, Hardee was reunited with his children when Anna brought them to West Point. They were to remain there until the fall of 1860, when Hardee received orders that he was to take a leave of absence until February 1861, when he would return to the First Cavalry regiment as a lieutenant colonel. During this time, however, the secession conventions were taking place, and when Georgia seceded in January 1861, Hardee resigned his commission.

The first year of the war was a successful one for Hardee in terms of status. In June 1861, he was named a brigadier general in the Confederate army. On October 7, he was promoted to major general. Also in 1861, Hardee's military academy textbook, *Rifle and Light Infantry Tactics*, was published. This went on to be a standard book used by both sides during the war. By October 1862, Hardee had been promoted to lieutenant general.

Unfortunately for his family, things were not looking so good in St. Augustine. By December 1861, the blockade and the large family were having their effect on the Dummett household: "Poor Anna, has the charge of a large family and is much perplexed as to what to do—her mother so infirm, so many children—the Madisons and Hardees—and quite a number of young darkies. She says what shall I do, I am out of corn—have been all around, can find only a small quantity at two dollars a bushel."[111] From Hardee's own letters, though, it appears that the family did not stay in the city for long. He claims his daughter Sallie took part in the chopping down of the flagpole in March 1862: "[She] struck the first blow…saying that the Stars & Stripes should not float from that Staff." Soon thereafter, the Hardee family and Anna Dummett left the city, taking residence in Orange Springs, Florida.[112]

General Hardee served in the western theater of the war and participated in many of the major battles there. Near the beginning of the war, he was charged with raising a brigade in Arkansas. He commanded the brigade until called to division command under General Albert Sydney Johnston in Kentucky and Tennessee. From there, he became a corps commander at Shiloh, where he was wounded while leading the first line of attack. He later led troops during the failed Kentucky campaign at Perryville, Murfreesboro and Missionary Ridge, among others. He served as a corps commander during the battles of the Atlanta campaign, with fighting being done at Reseca, Kennesaw Mountain, Peachtree Creek and Jonesboro. Hardee was then assigned command of the Department of South Carolina, Georgia and

The Battle of Kennesaw Mountain, in which William J. Hardee led troops, proved to be a rare Confederate victory during Sherman's 1864 Atlanta Campaign. Original print by Kurz and Allison. *Courtesy Library of Congress.*

Florida. In this role, he helped organize the retreat from Savannah, through Charleston and to Columbia, South Carolina, in advance of William T. Sherman's troops. During the Battle of Bentonville in North Carolina, Hardee's young son was to fall dead among the approximately 240 men the Confederates lost.

During his career, soldiers always knew they could count on Hardee as their leader. They bestowed on him the nickname "Old Reliable," a name that is still used when talking about him.

During the war, Hardee met Mary Lewis, and the two were wed in January 1863. Mary came from a wealthy background, and it was on property she brought to the marriage that Hardee worked as a planter after the war. In February 1866, Hardee was named president of the Selma and Meridian Railroad. As with almost all infrastructure in the South after the war, this railroad was in dire straits. Hardee worked just as hard at the rail business as he had while a general. He obtained loans; purchased engines, including several from the United States government; and worked to improve tracks and bring rail travel and transport back to the area. Unfortunately, the economic situation was too desperate, and by 1868, the venture went into receivership, eventually being sold to a New York firm.

Hardee eventually received his pardon from the United States and lived out his life in relative ease. He made visits to St. Augustine to see family and also to family property in White Sulphur Springs, West Virginia. During a trip to West Virginia in 1873, Hardee fell desperately sick and eventually passed away in Wytheville, Virginia, on November 6, 1873. While the cause of death is not known for certain, Hardee was still a relatively young man, not having reached the age of sixty. His prior stomach problems have led some to speculate he may have had stomach cancer. What we do know is that Hardee's remains were returned to Selma, Alabama, and he was buried in Live Oak Cemetery.[113]

MARTIN D. HARDIN

Martin Davis Hardin was born on June 26, 1837, in Jacksonville, Illinois. His grandfather was a U.S. senator from Kentucky with the same name, and his father was Major General John J. Hardin, who lost his life at the Battle of Buena Vista during the Mexican War. In 1851, his mother, Sarah, married Reuben Hyde Walworth. Walworth, a devout Catholic and last chancellor of the state of New York, moved the family to his Pine Grove estate in Saratoga Springs, New York. Sarah would later convert and become Roman Catholic. It was Walworth who helped the young Hardin get into the U.S. Military Academy and then later pushed his career behind the scenes:

> *My step son Lieut. Martin D. Hardin of the 3d regiment of U.S. Artillery, the oldest son of your deceased friend Col. John J. Hardin who fell at Buena Vista, has just returned from Oregon, where he has been stationed for some time, & is as I understand now at Washington, or in its vicinity, with his company.*
>
> *In June 1854 I got him in, as a cadet at large, at West Point; where he was an officer of the cadet corps nearly the whole time he was there. He graduated with much credit, & high up in his class, and I have no doubt he is one of the best and most reliable officers of his age in the army. Previous to the breaking out of the rebellion he had, with my concurrence & approbation, determined to leave the army, & to become a lawyer. But before he left California he wrote to his mother that he considered it his duty*

to continue to serve his country in the army until the termination of the war; before he commenced the study of the law.

...I am desirous that he should at once obtain a higher situation than that of a first lieut. in the Army; where he may not only be useful to his country but may also acquire reputation, while he is receiving such pay as to be able to lay by the means of educating himself for the law when the war is at an end. I know he is brave, as his father was, and will not spare himself but court danger. And I fear that if he stays in his present situation as a lieutenant of artillery his life will be unnecessarily sacrificed; or if he survives will neither acquire reputation or the means of future support.[111]

Martin D. Hardin served as a major general during the Civil War, losing an arm at Catlett's Station. During retirement, he was popular in the social scene of St. Augustine. *Courtesy Library of Congress.*

Martin D. Hardin served under Robert E. Lee and was present for the capture and hanging of John Brown. Illustration originally in *Frank Leslie's Illustrated Newspaper* 9, no. 211 (December 17, 1859): 33. *Courtesy Library of Congress.*

Hardin graduated from West Point in 1859. He served under the command of Robert E. Lee and was present at Harpers Ferry for the capture and hanging of John Brown. After this, he spent time in the Oregon Territory, serving as a lieutenant in the artillery before returning east at the outset of the Civil War.

During the Peninsula Campaign, Hardin served as an aide to Henry J. Hunt, the chief of George McClellan's reserve artillery. He was wounded twice at Second Manassas. For his actions, he received brevets to captain and major.

It was in September 1862 that Hardin was named colonel of the Twelfth Pennsylvania Reserve Volunteers. While colonel, he led his men at the Battle of Gettysburg, at Bristoe Station and later during the Mine Run campaign. It was during the Mine Run campaign that Hardin was severely injured. While at Catlett's Station inspecting troops, they were attacked by Confederate guerrillas, and Hardin lost his left arm. An obituary for Hardin claims the attack was made by John S. Mosby and his men. By the spring of 1864, Hardin was back with his troops for the Battle of Spotsylvania. He would again be wounded during the Battle of North Anna just days later.

Henry J. Hunt was chief of reserve artillery under George McClellan. *Courtesy Library of Congress.*

His bravery and dedication led to several more brevets and, finally, the promotion to brigadier general of volunteers.

Hardin was mustered out of the volunteer service in early 1866 and was given the rank of major in the Forty-third Infantry of the regular army. He retired in 1870 with the rank of brigadier general "for disability from wounds and loss of an arm in battle."

Still a young man, Hardin took to the study of law and was quickly admitted to the bar of Illinois. He practiced law for many years in the Chicago area. It was during this time that he and his first wife, Estelle Graham Hardin, began to visit St. Augustine during the winters. The Hardins leased the Tovar House located on St. Francis Street from Mrs. Francis M. von Balsam for a period of ten years. Mrs. Hardin had been sick for several years and accompanied the general south each year. General Hardin was said to have shown her much devotion and care. Mrs. Hardin passed away in 1890 at the age of forty-three.[115]

Despite his loss, General Hardin continued to winter in St. Augustine. His arrival each year was met with much fanfare, as in 1891: "General M.D. Hardin, one of our honored citizens, is again among us, much to the delight of old and young. The General is one of our soldier boys, of whom we are justly proud—a pride the whole country shares with us." And again in 1892: "General Martin D. Hardin, United States army, retired, has returned for another winter at his old home on St. Francis Street, much to the pleasure of the army colony and other friends here who feared that when the gallant veteran left last fall he would not again return."[116]

The Hardin home, which had received many upgrades from its famous resident, was a center of social activity. In 1892, when he had company, the *Tatler* reported:

> *General M.D. Hardin has with him at his cottage on St. Francis Street his sister, Mrs. E.H. Walworth, a prominent member of the Daughters of the Revolution, and her daughter, Miss R.H. Walworth, a clever young lady, who with Miss Bessie Ranney of Elizabeth, NY and Miss E.J. Hardin, of Fort Hamilton, form a coterie of "maidens fair to see" and a great addition to the society of this city. Mrs. Frazier of the Valencia caters to them.*[117]

While in town that year, Ellen Hardin Walworth composed a poem about the house that was published in the *Tatler*:

> *Casa Del Canonasa**
> *Without my window's fair expanse,*
> *Spread southern skies of deepest blue,*
> *And drifting clouds the scene enhance,*
> *Above the bay of azure hue.*
> *Close by the window's ledge are seen,*
> *A hundred golden balls that bend*
> *Beneath their leaves of glistening green,*
> *And orange blooms their odors lend.*
> *'Twixt tree and bay the barracks stand*
> *Where monks their quiet cloister reared;*
> *Now soldiers' tread and martial band*
> *Sound where the veeper song was heard.*
> *The wand of modern life has cast*
> *Its spell o'er convent hall and court,*
> *As high the flagstaff like a mast,*
> *Flings from its shaft the flag in sport.*
> *And stern the evening gun reports*
> *The day expired, for good or ill,*
> *While echoes vibrate from old forts,*
> *That of past ages whisper still.*
> **When this old coquina house was renovated a few year ago by General H— for use as a private cottage, two cannon balls of the very old Spanish time were found imbedded in the walls, hence its name.*[118]

The special visit from his sister also called for a special party, and the one given was called "one of the prettiest parties given in this city, in recent years." The Hardin home was "artistically decorated, and a table loaded with delicacies, delicious salads, dainty sandwiches, coffee. Ices and cake served by the gentlemen present were enjoyed, the quaint rooms admired and the General complimented on his great generalship in arranging so elegant an entertainment." The guest list at the party was extensive, including family, friends and officers from the St. Francis Barracks.[119]

Conspicuously absent on the guest list was Amelia McLaughlin, whom Hardin was to marry in October 1892 while in Chicago. Amelia was born in July 1864, making her twenty-seven years Martin's junior. She was the daughter of William and Mary McLaughlin of Chicago. The Hardins split their time between Chicago and St. Augustine, being active in both locations. Martin was still playing golf, a game he loved despite his physical limitations, until at least 1908 at the age of seventy-one.[120]

In 1916, the Hardins moved across town into what later was called the Generals House, so called because John Schofield had lived in the house prior. When Martin D. Hardin passed away at his home on December 12, 1923, there was a distinct sadness in the city. The local newspaper published several announcements and had a detailed article covering the Hardin funeral. The procession was a large one:

> *The funeral cortege left the family residence on Valencia Street shortly before 10 o'clock and scores of autos were in line, with representatives of many organizations walking in the procession. First came the military escort, then the hearse, the active and honorary pallbearers, cars containing the family, and the last little remnant of the local post of the Grand Army of the Republic, fellow comrads of the deceased. There followed delegations from the Spanish War Veterans, American Legion, Boy Scouts, Knights of Columbus, American Legion Auxiliary, Catholic Relief Association and other organizations, with scores of private citizens who joined in the tribute of respect.*[121]

General Hardin was buried in St. Augustine National Cemetery rather than Arlington at the request of his wife, Amelia. She felt that because of his love for the city he should be buried there.

In the years following General Hardin's death, Amelia continued to live in the city, oftentimes taking part in philanthropic activities. Perhaps her most lasting gift was in memory of her husband. On the property of

Nombre de Dios, Mrs. Hardin was responsible for restoring and furnishing the small chapel on the grounds. A small plaque at the entry marks her gift: "In memoriam General M.D. Hardin I have loved O Lord the beauty of thy house and the place where thy glory dwelleth."[122]

Amelia Hardin died on November 29, 1939, and is buried alongside her husband in St. Augustine National Cemetery.

William Wing Loring

William Wing Loring was neither born in nor died in St. Augustine, yet his memory is woven into the fabric of the city. Loring was born in Wilmington, North Carolina, on December 4, 1818, to Reuben and Hannah Kenan Loring. The Loring family moved to St. Augustine in 1823, living on St. George Street, and acquired an orange grove located on Julington Creek. Reuben was also apparently a builder of some reputation and was contracted to build a sugar mill for Thomas Dummett, the father-in-law of William Hardee, on land located between St. Augustine and Ormond Beach. Also showing how close-knit the community was at the time, in 1833, Reuben hosted a retirement dinner for Judge Joseph L. Smith, the father of future Confederate general Edmund Kirby Smith.[123]

Early on, Loring led the life of a soldier. In 1832, at just fourteen years old, he volunteered for service, earning himself the nickname "Boy Soldier." He served in the Florida Militia during the Indian Wars, fighting in several battles before earning a promotion to second lieutenant in 1837. Afterward, he was sent to the Alexandria Boarding School in Virginia and then studied law at Georgetown College. He later returned to Florida and in 1842 began practicing law in St. Augustine. He served from 1842 to 1845 in the Florida legislature.

In 1846, Loring returned to military life by joining the Mounted Riflemen, a regiment authorized by Congress to help protect the Oregon Territory. The regiment was sent to join General Winfield Scott in the invasion of Mexico in 1847. It was during the Battle of Chapultepec near the Belan gate that Loring suffered a severe wound in his arm that ultimately required its amputation. The report of the surgery is that of legend: "Loring laid aside a cigar, sat quietly in a chair without opiates to relieve the pain, and allowed the arm to be cut off without a murmur or a groan. The arm was buried on the heights by his men, with the hand pointing towards the City of Mexico."[124]

From "boy soldier" to serving as a general in the Egyptian army, William Loring had a military career spanning fifty years. *Courtesy State Archives of Florida.*

His actions led to a promotion to the rank of brevet colonel. Upon returning to Florida in December 1847, the state House and Senate passed a resolution of appreciation for both Loring and Lieutenant Mathias C. Marin.

Over the next years, Loring spent time in the Oregon Territory. During the California gold rush, Loring had to deal with the problem of soldiers deserting their post. In March 1850, approximately 150 men left in hopes of striking it rich. Loring and his men were able to capture 73 of the men. In the coming years, Loring and his troops were sent to Texas to deal with the "Indian problem" and later back west to Utah to participate in the growing concern with the Mormon religion that was now based there.

Lieutenant John Dubois was correct when he wrote about Loring, "I doubt Loring's loyalty, but he says he is sound."[125] Loring resigned from the Union army in June 1861. Within months of his appointment as brigadier general in the Confederate army, Loring was feuding with Thomas "Stonewall" Jackson when Jackson abandoned the winter campaign, taking his troops to quarters in Winchester, Virginia. Loring and his men were left to defend Romney but without the needed supplies to fight the cold winter. This issue was sent to Richmond, where Secretary of War Judah Benjamin ordered Jackson to order Loring to Winchester. Jackson did so but under protest and threat of resignation. Jackson then brought charges against Loring for neglect of duty. Rather than face court-martial, Loring was instead promoted to major general. The commands were eventually separated entirely, and Loring was ordered to take charge of the Department of Southwest Virginia.

It was during the siege at Vicksburg that Loring earned his nickname "Old Blizzards." While facing Union gunboats at Fort Pemberton on the Yazoo River, Loring is said to have stood on the breastworks yelling, "Give them blizzards, boys! Give them blizzards!" His artillery fought well that day and repulsed several ships out of range.[126]

Later in the war, Loring served under Leonidas Polk in the Atlanta Campaign. When Polk was killed on June 14, 1864, Loring temporarily acted as commander of the Army of Tennessee, serving under Joseph Johnston. When Johnston was relieved of command in favor of General John Bell Hood, Loring was returned to division command under new commander Alexander P. Stewart. After Hood's dismal showing at Atlanta, the troops were forced to retreat, with Loring's division the last to leave.

Alexander P. Stewart served in the western theater of the war, rising to the rank of lieutenant general. His pre- and postwar years were spent in academics, finally serving as chancellor at the University of Mississippi. *Courtesy Library of Congress.*

After the war, based on the recommendation of William Sherman, the Khedive of Egypt hired Loring as one of twenty new officers for his army. Khedives were Egyptian rulers from 1867 to 1914, serving as a viceroy of the sultan of Turkey. In 1869, Loring was named inspector general of the army. While he was able to get along well with troops, he and other Americans were unable to grasp the religious devoutness of the Muslim men, and Loring himself never mastered the Arabic language. While serving in Egypt, Loring was able to reacquaint himself with General Ulysses S. Grant, with whom he had fought in Mexico many years before.

Grant was on his post-presidential world tour and dined with many former soldiers from the Civil War. The animosity of prior years had long passed for these men.

Loring left Egypt in 1879, arriving in New York City for a family visit before returning to St. Augustine. He arrived to great fanfare and honors. He was met at the train depot by Mayor H.F. Oliveros, St. Johns County commissioner Bartolo Genovar, the St. Augustine Brass Band and many others. Near the Confederate monument, Mayor Oliveros said a few words: "General Loring, today St. Augustine welcomes home one of her noblest sons. The compliment of welcoming you has been extended to me as a native born citizen, grown to manhood since your absence. We greet you with open arms and happy hearts. General, this is no welcome to a hero, nor a statesman, nor one aspiring to public honors, but sir, we welcome you as a humble citizen of St. Augustine, after a separation of thirty years."[127]

From 1880 through Loring's death in December 1886, he lived in New York City but made annual visits to his adopted hometown. It was during this time that he published his memoirs of his time in Egypt: *A Confederate Soldier in Egypt*. His planned autobiography for the rest of his life was never completed.

William W. Loring passed away on December 20, 1886, in New York City after a very brief illness. According to the *New York Times* obituary, General Loring was cremated and buried at Grace Episcopal Church. His remains were not to stay there long, however. In March 1887, the *Florida Times-Union* carried a long notice regarding Loring's remains being moved to St. Augustine. The Slave Market in the Plaza was used for the start of the procession. The floral arrangements were said to be "of a degree of perfection and profusion that is seldom excelled…By the time the people began to pour into the historic building where the remains lay, the lid and sides of the casket and also the bier, had been converted into a magnificent bed of flowers, the colors blended in perfect harmony, and which completely obscured the black pall from view." The funeral procession made its way through the old streets to the cemetery approximately a mile and a half away. Loring's remains joined those of Randolph Caldecott as the most famous burials in Woodlawn Cemetery. The burial of William Loring served to help remind everybody present of the progress that had been made between North and South:

> *After the return from the cemetery, the veterans of the Posts and Camp held a reunion or jubilee at Genovar's Opera House. The old battle cries*

were made to resound again, and the exchange of friendly sentiments was followed by cheers. The Federals gave three cheers for the Confederates and the latter returned the compliment by giving three cheers to the Federals, then all joined in three cheers for the National Flag. Speeches and handshaking closed the jubilee.

The saga of William Loring's remains was not to end here, however. In 1920, the Anna Dummett Chapter of the United Daughters of the Confederacy and the General Loring Chapter of the Children of the Confederacy began raising funds for what they thought to be a more fitting monument to the general. A fifteen-square-foot plot in the Plaza was granted to them, and on July 6, 1920, the ashes of William Loring were moved to their final resting place in downtown St. Augustine.[128]

JOHN M. SCHOFIELD

John McAllister Schofield was born in Gerry, New York, on September 29, 1831. In 1849, he received an appointment to the United States Military Academy and graduated seventh in his class in 1853. He then served in the artillery for two years before returning to West Point

Union major general John M. Schofield was a regular visitor to St. Augustine and was a popular subject of the local society pages in the newspaper. *Courtesy Library of Congress.*

as an instructor. In 1859–60, he was on leave from the military and served as a professor of physics at Washington University in St. Louis.

When the war broke out, Schofield served as a major in the First Missouri Infantry. He was then chief of staff to Major General Nathaniel Lyon during the Battle of Wilson's Creek. Schofield quickly earned promotions to brigadier general in November 1861 with command of all Union militia in Missouri and then to major general in November 1862. His promotion to major general was not approved until May 1863, however. He was then in command of the Department of the Missouri. In 1864, he was in command of the Army of the Ohio and fought during William Sherman's Atlanta Campaign.

After the fall of Atlanta, Schofield and his men were sent to serve under Major General George H. Thomas in Tennessee. It was here that they achieved victories over Confederate general John Bell Hood at the Battles of Franklin and Nashville. All was not well between Thomas and Schofield, however, as tensions arose from Schofield's time as a student at West Point. Thomas had voted to expel Schofield over claims that he had allowed younger cadets to make offensive jokes while he was serving as a teaching assistant in the mathematics department. While he was not expelled, it would stand to reason that attempts made by Schofield to wrest control of this army from Thomas would stem from this earlier incident.

Major General George H. Thomas is often known by his nickname, the "Rock of Chickamauga." *Courtesy Library of Congress.*

Nothing came of Schofield's ploy, but he did receive a promotion to brigadier general in the regular army for his on-the-field actions. In March 1865, serving as the commander of the Department of North Carolina, he was again linked with Sherman in a campaign that culminated with the surrender of Confederate troops under command of Joseph Johnston.

In 1868, Schofield was named secretary of war under President Andrew Johnson. He resigned this position once

Ulysses S. Grant was elected, instead opting to return to the army in the position of major general. In 1873, Schofield penned a report for then Secretary of War William Belknap recommending the use of Pearl Harbor as a naval base. By 1876, he was serving as superintendent at West Point, a position he would hold until a scandal involving a black cadet led to his removal in 1881. This scandal did little to hurt Schofield's career, however, and in 1888, he was appointed commanding general of the United States. He held this position until his mandatory retirement at age sixty-four in 1895. Schofield retired with the rank of lieutenant general.[129]

General Schofield and his wife were frequent winter guests in St. Augustine, and his visits were always chronicled by the local press. In 1891, they stayed at the Hotel Ponce de Leon, while in 1896, they were visitors at the Alcazar Hotel. In 1897, perhaps looking for more privacy, they rented a home at 7 Carrera Street:

> *Lieutenant General and Mrs. Schofield are spending the winter in St. Augustine, occupying one of the Ponce de Leon cottages on Carrera Street. The General is enjoying a well-earned rest after years of active service. The rest, however, is by no means an idle one, as he is compiling a book of his army experience, and at the same time contributing to the "Century," Mrs. Schofield assisting in many ways. She is very fond of St. Augustine, and is thoroughly enjoying her home, its quiet and freedom from the care that a large establishment entailed, while St. Augustine's pride in having General and Mrs. Schofield with them is exceedingly pleasant.*[130]

Despite the *Tatler*'s comments regarding a smaller home, the Schofields took up residence at a much larger house located at 20 Valencia Street in 1899. This is possibly due to the birth of a daughter to the general and his much younger wife, Georgia. A 1900 report is given of a birthday party held at the Valencia Street residence: "Miss Georgina Schofield celebrated the third anniversary of her birthday very prettily on March fourth, at the home of her parents, General and Mrs. John M. Schofield on Valencia Street." In 1901, the home was being enlarged: "A two-story brick addition to General Schofield's residence on Valencia Street is in course of erection. The new wing is on the west side of the building."[131]

On March 5, 1906, John M. Schofield died at his home in St. Augustine as the result of a cerebral hemorrhage. He received a respectful obituary in the local newspaper: "General Schofield's death was a great shock to the community as his illness had been brief, and few outside of close personal friends were aware of his indisposition. Prior to Friday he had been around as usual on the streets and seemed to be enjoying normal health." General Schofield was buried with military honors in Arlington National Cemetery.[132]

Edmund Kirby Smith

Perhaps the most famous of generals to have close ties to St. Augustine may also have the fewest number of ties. Edmund Kirby Smith was born on May 16, 1824, in the Segui House to parents Joseph Lee Smith and Frances Kirby. Anecdotally, Edmund was the first child to be baptized at Trinity Episcopal Church. While the majority of St. Augustine residents were Catholic, the Smiths were proud Episcopalians. Edmund, however, was not so fond of attending services. His older sister Frances, who was his primary caregiver, was forced to wield a firm hand in making him attend.

In 1836, young Edmund was sent to Benjamin Hollowell's school in Alexandria, Virginia. Hollowell's was seen as excellent preparation for admission to the Academy at West Point. Smith had a good academic record while in Virginia, and in 1841, he received his appointment. Smith received the nickname "Seminole" while at West Point. This was not due to anything he did but rather because he was from Florida and the publicity surrounding the Seminole War. Edmund graduated twenty-fifth in his class and was commissioned a brevet second lieutenant and assigned to the Fifth Infantry Regiment and began preparations to head west under General Zachary Taylor.[133]

During the Mexican War, Smith served under General Taylor at the Battles of Palo Alto and Reseca de la Palma. Under General Winfield Scott, he received brevet promotions to first lieutenant and, later, captain for his actions at Contreras and Churubusco.

After the Mexican War, Smith served as a professor of mathematics at West Point before returning to active service fighting Indians in the Texas frontier. By 1861, Smith had been promoted to major in the Second Cavalry. It was here that he refused to surrender his men and Fort Colorado to the Texas militia under the command of Ben McCullough. Smith had a change of heart, however, and resigned his commission on April 6, 1861, joining his native state of Florida.

Smith and his abilities were quickly recognized, and he was commissioned a lieutenant colonel under the command of Joseph Johnston. By June, Smith had been promoted to brigadier general, commanding a brigade in the Army of the Shenandoah. In July, his brigade saw its first combat at the Battle of First Bull Run. It was here that Smith was injured in the shoulder. While recuperating, Smith met a young woman by the name of Cassie Selden, who by mid-September was to become his wife. Their first daughter was born in 1862, and they later had ten other children, all of whom lived to adulthood.

General Edmund Kirby Smith was one of the last Confederate generals to surrender to Union forces. *Courtesy Library of Congress.*

October 1861 saw Smith back in the army, now at the rank of major general. By 1862, his star continued to shine, and he was in command of the District of East Tennessee. Here he served under Braxton Bragg and during the Kentucky campaign scored a victory at the Battle of Richmond on August 30. For this, he was again promoted on October 9, this time to the rank of lieutenant general

January 1863 saw Smith transferred farther west, where he was named commander of the Trans-Mississippi Department. Here he was far from the political eyes of Richmond but also became physically cut off after the success of Ulysses S. Grant in taking control of the Mississippi River. All was not completely lost, however, and Smith's men scored a considerable victory at the Battle of Mansfield during the Red River Campaign in 1864. As things continued to deteriorate for the Confederacy, Smith was not immune. He attempted to send forces east, but Union control of the Mississippi thwarted his efforts. An attempted invasion of Missouri met with failure as well. Smith found himself the last major Confederate army still on the field and in May 1865 began surrender negotiations before finally signing the formal documents on June 2, 1865, near Galveston. Despite the fact that the war was over and Smith had little option but to surrender, there were those who wanted to continue fighting. The *Texas Republican*, out of Marshall, laid the blame squarely on Smith, calling him a poor administrator and saying that the troops had lost confidence in him.[134]

Fearing arrest, Smith and many other Confederates made their way to Mexico. Smith reached Mexico City by mid-July. Still not assured of safety, he continued on, reaching Cuba on July 28. Here he met Judah Benjamin and many other Confederate escapees. By November, however, Smith was back on United States soil and took the amnesty oath on November 14, 1865.

Smith had a busy postwar life as president first at Accident Insurance Company and later the Atlantic and Pacific Telegraph Company. Both jobs ended in failure. From 1870 to 1875, Smith worked as a professor at the University of Nashville. Here he taught mental philosophy, political economy, natural history, geology and agriculture. In 1875, the college became the State Normal College, and Smith was again looking for work. He was appointed professor of mathematics at the University of the South in Sewanee, Tennessee. Smith was considered to be a good math teacher but not a mathematician. He continued in his role of professor until his death in 1893.

Edmund Kirby Smith does not appear to have spent a major amount of time in Florida after leaving for West Point. He and his sister sold his birth home in 1887, and it was used as a boardinghouse. In 1895, the building was donated in trust to become the free library for the city and is currently entrusted to the St. Augustine Historical Society and houses its extensive library.

On March 28, 1893, Smith passed away in Sewanee, Tennessee, after a brief illness. His burial took place at the University of the South Cemetery.[135]

Despite not having lived in the state for years, he was still considered a state hero. Smith is immortalized as part of the National Statuary Hall Collection located in the Capital Building in Washington, D.C. Here, each state is granted the right to donate two statues of individuals of historic importance to the state. The bronze statue of Edmund Kirby Smith was created by St. Augustine artist C. Adrian Pillars and placed in 1922. It currently stands in the Capital Visitor Center for all to see.[136]

Chapter 7

A Walking and Driving Tour of Civil War–Related Sites

Most tours of St. Augustine will at best briefly mention the Civil War. While it is true that little of military importance happened here, the city itself played an important role in the Union efforts to control blockade runners and hamper Confederate supply efforts. The city contains numerous sites of interest to those concerned with the Civil War, and these walking and driving tours will lead you to many of them.

Due to some of the distances involved and also the fact that the area becomes exceedingly hot and humid, I have created two separate walking tours. Each covers a separate area of the city and will allow you to better focus your time and energies. After the two walking tours, I have included other points of interest for those interested in the Civil War. In general, these are a little more out of the way than the other tours.

Where possible, I have included addresses, GPS coordinates and website information. I believe that this will help visitors gather information, more easily navigate the city and find locations that will most interest them.

Tour One

Visitor Information Center

10 South Castillo Drive
N29°53.915 W081°18.863
Located at the corner of San Marco Avenue and Castillo Drive across from Ripley's Believe It or Not

While the starting point does not have any Civil War association, it is a must-see for anybody visiting St. Augustine. The Visitor Center has a convenient parking garage, which you will find to be a blessing after driving around the city for a few minutes. Parking in St. Augustine is at a premium, and the cost is well worth it, especially during the hot summer months.

Inside the Visitor Information Center, you will find a large assortment of information on the city. Brochures for hotels, restaurants, attractions, shopping and more are available. Be sure to grab a city map. There is also a small but well-stocked gift shop with an assortment of just about everything. The book room is usually well stocked and worth a look. If you didn't bring sunscreen or water, have no fears; they are available. During the heat of the day, you will need both. Clean restrooms are also available.

Directions—Upon leaving the Visitor Center, you should now be facing east. You will see the Huguenot Cemetery on your left-hand side. Walk straight ahead until you reach Orange Street. To the right, you will see a building that currently is home to the Old Drug Store and Potter's Wax Museum. This will be Cordova Street. Follow along Cordova until on the right you will come to

Tolomato Cemetery

N29°53.820 W081°18.889
www.tolomatocemetery.com

Now owned by the Cathedral-Basilica of St. Augustine, Tolomato Cemetery is the oldest planned cemetery in Florida, with known plans going back to 1811. More than one thousand known burials are located within the stone walls; however, many have been lost to time and the elements. The cemetery is open for viewing only limited days and hours, so please check the website if you are interested in walking the grounds. If it is not open, you are still able to see the main points of interest while looking through the fence.

Located in the center walkway, you will find the resting spot of Bishop Augustin Verot. Verot was the third bishop of Savannah, later becoming the first bishop of St. Augustine. Verot is known for his anti-abolition sermons, preferring to allow slavery to die its own death. He later became a Reconstruction leader in the educating of the newly freed black children. He played a vital role in bringing the Sisters of St. Joseph from Le Puy, France, to St. Augustine and, later, Savannah, Georgia.

When facing the back of the cemetery, on the left, be sure to note the lineup of eleven Veterans' Administration headstones honoring Confederate soldiers buried in Tolomato Cemetery. Cemetery information shows these headstones were placed in 2000. All eleven men served in Florida Infantry brigades, with just over half having served in the St. Augustine Blues. Also, be sure to notice that most of these men are of Minorcan decent. Also of interest to Civil War enthusiasts would be the graves of members of the United States Colored Troops. They are located near the entry gate on the right-hand side.

If the cemetery is open, it is worth walking through. In the very back, you will find the Varela Chapel. This was originally built for Father Felix Varela, a Cuban-born priest. Upon the death of Bishop Verot, his remains were put in the chapel as well. In 1911, Varela's remains were returned to Cuba, and he was reinterred at the University of Havana. The remains of Bishop Verot were moved to their current location in 1985. The chapel is now used on occasion for a special Mass. Also buried in the cemetery is Father Miguel O'Reilly, the first pastor of what is now the St. Augustine Cathedral. Father Michael Crosby, O'Reilly's successor, is also buried in Tolomato. Lost to time are the graves of nineteenth-century Haitian revolutionary General Biassou and several members of the Sisters of St. Joseph.

Directions—Turn left out of the cemetery back on to Cordova Street and walk about a block until you come to Tolomato Lane. Turn right here and follow along until you get to St. George Street. St. George Street is what many people think of when they think of St. Augustine. There are all kinds of shops and places to eat and occasionally a little bit of history thrown in. When you get to St. George Street, turn right. Follow along until on the right-hand side you will come to

Arrivas House (now home to the Panama Hat Company)

46 St. George Street

The Arrivas House was originally constructed around 1740. During the Civil War, the house was the residence of Paul Arnau. Arnau was the St. Augustine collector of customs and superintendent of lighthouses. In January 1861, he helped carry out Confederate government orders by darkening and later removing the lighting fixtures of the St. Augustine Lighthouse. He also helped in the darkening of the lighthouses at Cape Canaveral, Jupiter Inlet and Cape Florida. Arnau was elected mayor of St. Augustine in November 1861 but quickly resigned this post in March 1862 rather than turning the city over to Union soldiers. The Union navy later arrested Arnau and held him until missing pieces from the various lighthouses were returned. Paul Arnau died in 1886 and is buried in Evergreen Cemetery. The only historical marker on the building states that the building is recognized as a restored colonial structure by the City of St. Augustine.

Directions—Turn around and head back toward Tolomato Lane. On the right-hand side you will come to Fort Alley. Turn right here and walk toward the very busy Castillo Drive. At the light, cross Castillo Drive and you will be arriving at

Castillo de San Marcos/Fort Marion

11 South Castillo Drive
www.nps.gov/casa/index.htm

When the city of St. Augustine comes up in conversation, the Castillo is generally the first place that people think about, and with good reason. The Castillo—as it is most commonly called today, rather than Fort Marion, as it was known during the Civil War—was built during the years 1672–95. The Castillo is made of coquina, a sedimentary rock made from periwinkle shells, oyster shells, limestone and other small rocks and shells that bond together to form the stone. The coquina used was quarried on Anastasia Island and shipped across the Matanzas River by ferry. When freshly dug, coquina is relatively pliable and can be shaped as needed. Once the coquina had been shaped and put into place, the sun dried it,

Fort Marion, or as it is more commonly called Castillo de San Marcos, was built by the Spanish between the years 1672 and 1695. *Courtesy Library of Congress.*

allowing it to become an excellent material for protecting an army or the citizens of the area. The Castillo walls are from fourteen to nineteen feet thick at the base tapering to approximately nine feet thick at the top. The coquina walls were able to absorb cannon shot and not explode and crumble like other forts.

Besides being built at a strategic defensive location for the city, the fort has four bastions, the roughly diamond-shaped corners. These bastions are named San Pedro, San Agustin, San Carlos and San Pablo. Bastions are more effective from a defensive point of view than building towers. Bastions allow the defender to be able to cover a wide area with cannon fire. Also included with the bastions was a several-foot-wide moat that could be filled with water from the river. The ground outside the moat was elevated and then gradually angled down. This allowed for more accurate cannon fire from the fort and also made it more difficult for enemy fire to be effective.

During the Civil War, Fort Marion, as it was called at that time, changed hands twice without a shot being fired. Confederates took the fort during the first year, and Union forces captured the fort in 1862 when they occupied the city. While the fort served little purpose militarily, there were valid reasons for the Union to hold it and the city. Being located directly on the river, the fort offered little opportunity for blockade runners to use St. Augustine as a safe house. To get to the city, blockade runners would have to sail within easy distance of Federal cannons. Another key reason for controlling the city was to use it as a rest area for troops. Many of the regiments sent to the city were sent for the purpose of resting and regaining strength. Many soldiers wrote home commenting on the good fortune of being far from battle and being located in what was considered to be a healthy climate.

Visitors to the Castillo today are mostly treated to history from earlier periods, with the Civil War being an afterthought. This is still an excellent destination. On most days, there are weapons demonstrations, park service employees and volunteers in period costumes, video presentations and more. There are excellent views from the gun deck; however, you must be able to climb the period stairs to reach this. If there is lightning in the area, as often happens during Florida afternoons, the gun deck is closed in the interest of safety.

Directions—Leave the fort by the same way you arrived: crossing the light at Castillo Drive. Follow the sidewalk away from the river until reaching the corner of Castillo and St. George Streets. You will now be at

The City Gates

The corner of Orange Street, Castillo Drive and St. George Street

As part of the protection of the city, the Cubo Line was established first by the Spanish in reaction to the English siege of the city in 1702. The current gate opening was first put into place around 1740. Two wooden guardhouses allowed entry and exit along what would become known as La Leche Gate, since the road led to the Chapel of Our Lady of La Leche. In 1804, Spanish engineer Manuel de Hita suggested replacing the wooden guardhouses with one made of masonry. By 1809, the coquina gates now seen here were completed. Originally, there was a moat in this area, and a bridge was located to the north of the gates. In 1908, the moat was filled in. During the Civil War years, the gate was used to control access into and out

The city gate of St. Augustine was part of the Cubo Line that helped serve as a defense for the Spanish against the English. This line was begun in 1704. The gate columns that stand today date to approximately 1808 and are made of coquina. Original photograph by Samuel A. Cooley. *Courtesy Library of Congress.*

of the city for both troops and civilians. Photographer Samuel Cooley has left us several period photos of the gate, allowing us to see changes to the area and repairs that have been made.

Directions—Walk through the City Gates and carefully cross Orange Street. On the left you will be arriving at

Huguenot Cemetery

Corner of Orange Avenue and Castillo Drive (San Marco Avenue)
N29°53.897 W081°18.829

The Huguenot Cemetery was started as a result of the 1821 yellow fever epidemic. City leaders needed a burial ground for all Protestant denominations of Christians. Catholics were buried in the earlier-visited Tolomato Cemetery. Title to the land was transferred to the Trustees of the Presbyterian Church in 1832, and the cemetery was closed to new burials by the city in 1884. Today, the cemetery is cared for by the Friends of the Huguenot Cemetery.

The name "Huguenot" may be confusing to some, as the term generally refers to sixteenth- and seventeenth-century French Protestants who followed the writings of John Calvin. Rather, it is believed that the term came into use in St. Augustine in the 1830s as a way to describe non-Catholics.

The cemetery appears to be open at rather random times and is staffed by volunteers. When open, it is a beautiful and well-cared-for cemetery.

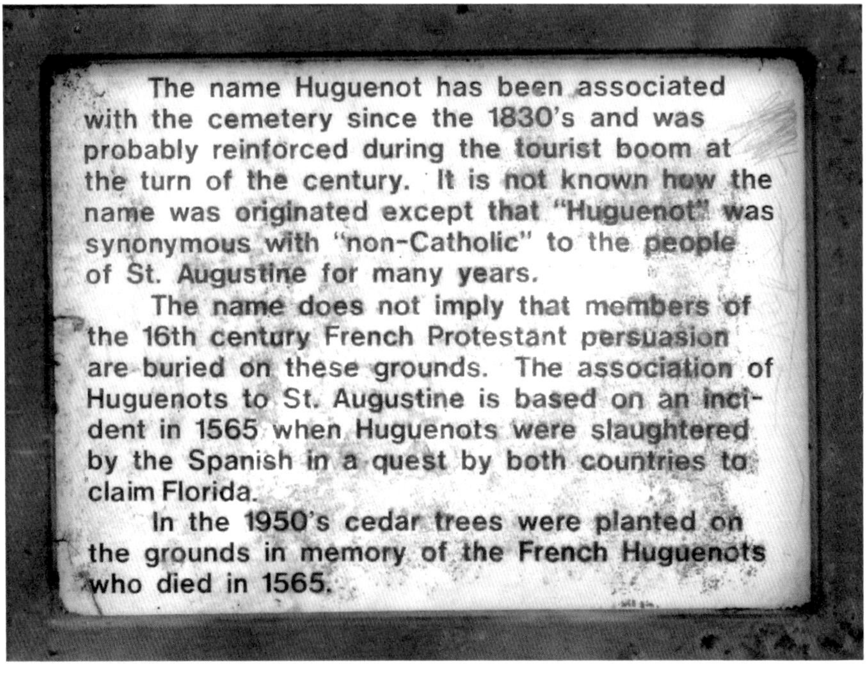

The historical marker at the entrance of the Huguenot Cemetery. *Courtesy the author.*

The volunteers are knowledgeable and more than willing to answer questions. After dark, the area outside the cemetery walls comes alive, as it is a popular stop on many of the ghost tours that roam the area.

There are four known burials of Confederate soldiers inside the cemetery walls. All served in various regiments of Florida Infantry. Also buried in the cemetery is Frances Kirby Smith, the outspoken Confederate mother of General Edmund Kirby Smith. Her small headstone is located almost directly ahead of the main gate along the back iron fence.

Tour Two

Plaza de la Constitucion

N29°53.556 W081°18.758

The Plaza was originally laid out by Spanish Royal Ordinances in 1573 less than ten years after the city was founded. These ordinances stated that the plaza should be in "good proportion—a prolonged square, the length equal to 1½ times the width." In the Plaza area are many historical markers worth stopping at: Prisoners of War during the American Revolution; Soldiers Killed during World War II, Korea and Vietnam; a reconstruction of an early 1800s well on an original well site; and the St. Augustine Foot Soldiers Monument honoring those who participated in the civil rights marches in the 1960s. Our first stop will be the

William Wing Loring Monument

N29°53.539 W081°18.828

William Wing Loring moved to St. Augustine with his family at the age of four. At fourteen, he began what became a fifty-year military career fighting under three different flags: the United States, the Confederacy and Egypt. In the United States Army, he achieved the rank of brevet colonel, in the Confederate army he achieved the rank of major general and in the Egyptian army he achieved the equivalent rank of major general. When Loring passed away in 1886, he was originally cremated

The William W. Loring memorial stands tall in the Plaza de la Constitucion, located in downtown St. Augustine. Loring's ashes were relocated here in 1920. *Courtesy the author.*

and buried in New York City but was reburied in St. Augustine early in 1887.

Loring was reinterred in the Plaza in 1920, and the current obelisk monument was erected a week later by the Anna Dummett Chapter of the United Daughters of the Confederacy.

Directions—Walk east toward the Matanzas River

Confederate Memorial

N29°53.550 W081°18.714

For an area that saw little firsthand of the war and for a city as small as St. Augustine, it sacrificed mightily. According to this memorial, no fewer than forty-four male citizens died in the war (see Appendix III).

The St. Augustine Confederate Memorial was originally located on property owned by the Catholic Church. The memorial was relocated to the Plaza de la Constitucion in 1879. *Courtesy State Archives of Florida.*

The Confederate Memorial was sponsored by the Ladies Memorial Association and spearheaded by Anna Dummett. The original monument was placed on Catholic Church property in 1872 after having been denied the right to place the monument on city property. After the era of Reconstruction, permission was granted for the monument to be placed in the Plaza, and it was rebuilt there in 1879.

Directions—Around you in the Plaza, you will notice several cannons. Be sure to stop and take a look at them.

Artillery Pieces

You will find two different types of artillery located in the Plaza. There are both eight-inch Columbiads and thirty-two-pound rifled cast-iron guns. Both types of guns have historical plaques associated with them. Historian Craig Swain, however, has put forth his doubts as to whether these guns could have actually seen action in St. Augustine during the war. While the evidence may prove the informative plaques wrong, these are still interesting pieces worth taking a look at. They will give you an idea of the type of weapons used during the war.

Directions—Continue east through the Plaza until you reach

The Public/Slave Market

Little arouses the ire of some folks more than the name of this structure. In general, the term "Public Market" is really most appropriate. The market area has been used for locals to sell their wares, mostly meats and vegetables, for years. In fact, still today you will find artisans selling their works from this central site.

The story of the "slave" market seems to have taken hold in the mid-1880s when mentioned in Bloomfield's Historical Guide and took off with the publication of a postcard by W.J. Harris with the name "Old Slave Market" on the back.

Local historian David Nolan has done research showing that there are known instances of slaves having been sold at the Public Market. While he does present documentary evidence, there is not enough to consider this a slave market in the way that those in Charleston or New Orleans were. This market was used as a true market, and only on rare occasion did slaves trade hands here.

Directions—Cross King Street and look for the arched entryway to Aviles Street. Turn south, and on the right-hand side you will arrive at

The Segui-Kirby Smith House

12 Aviles Street
N29°53.491 W081°18.694
www.staugustinehistoricalsociety.org/library.html

The Segui-Kirby Smith House dates to the 1700s, with the land having been occupied even longer. Bernardo Segui, who was of Minorcan descent, purchased the home in 1786. In 1823, the home was rented by Judge Joseph Lee Smith and his wife, Frances Kirby. In 1824, Edmund Kirby Smith was born in the home. Edmund graduated from West Point in 1845 before serving in the army in varying capacities. During the Civil War, he obtained the rank of full general in the Confederate army.

General Smith and his sister sold the home in 1887. In 1895, the building was purchased by John L. and Francis Wilson, who donated the building in trust to be used as a public library. The building is still used for this purpose and serves as the research library for the St. Augustine Historical Society. Directions—If the library is open, pass through the entry gate and into the garden area. You will find the sculpture

Sons of St. Augustine

This life-sized bronze sculpture recognizes the lives of two men from different backgrounds yet thrown together in life. Sculptor Maria Kirby-Smith, great-granddaughter of Edmund, has memorialized Edmund Kirby Smith and Dr. Alexander H. Darnes in a tribute fitting the deeds of both men. Darnes

The *Sons of St. Augustine* sculpture features Edmund Kirby Smith and Alexander Darnes. The sculpture was created by Maria Kirby-Smith, the great-granddaughter of Edmund Kirby Smith. *Courtesy the author.*

was a slave born into the Kirby Smith family after Edmund had departed for boarding school. Darnes, however, later accompanied Smith while he was a member of both the United States and Confederate armies. Darnes was not a member of either army.

The sculpture captures both men later in life portraying their postwar successes. Smith is shown in academic regalia suiting his career as a professor of mathematics at the University of the South at Sewanee. Dr. Darnes is shown with his medical bag, a reminder of the great services he provided his community of Jacksonville. Also highlighted is the Masonic symbol on his watch fob. Darnes was a prominent Mason and had served as Florida deputy grand master at the time of his death.

Directions—You will have two options for exiting the Segui-Kirby Smith House gardens: 1) Exit onto Artillery Lane and then turn left. Follow Artillery Lane until you reach St. George Street. Turn left on St. George, and be advised that this portion of St. George Street is open to traffic. OR 2) Exit through the same gate you entered by and turn right on Aviles Street. Continue approximately one block until reaching Cadiz Street. Turn right on Cadiz and follow for approximately one block until reaching St. George Street, where you will turn left.

Emancipation Proclamation Lot

238 St. George Street next to the Villa Flora building
N29°53.422 W081°18.737
www.ssjfl.org

Located across the street from the Sisters of St. Joseph Motherhouse is a plot of land that originally was the location of a Spanish chapel, Nuestra Senora de la Soledad. When the English took control of St. Augustine, the church was turned into the Anglican St. Peter's Church. Later, the Spanish returned, and in 1784, the building was torn down, with some of the materials being used in the building of the Catholic basilica now located next to the Plaza.

An oral account from 1934 claims that slaves were gathered together in this lot, the Emancipation Proclamation was read and freedom was granted to those previously enslaved. A descriptive plaque now marks the location of the former church and the location where slaves were given their freedom.

Oral history states that the lot where this marker is located is where slaves were gathered and granted their freedom in 1863. *Courtesy the author.*

Directions—Continue walking south on St. George Street. When you reach the corner of St. George Street and St. Francis Street, you will be at

St. Francis Inn (Dummett House)

279 St. George Street
N29°53.270 W081°18.679
www.stfrancisinn.com

Located on the picturesque corner of St. George and St. Francis Streets sits the St. Francis Inn. The inn has become one of St. Augustine's most famous bed-and-breakfasts.

The original Dummett family owner of the home was Thomas Henry Dummett, who purchased the property in October 1838. Thomas, a native of Barbados and a colonel in the British marines, passed away in August 1839, leaving the home to his widow, Mary. In 1845, the home passed to daughters Anna and Sarah. Anna used the property as a boardinghouse until title was transferred to future Confederate general William J. Hardee, Sarah's husband. Hardee is perhaps best known for having authored *Rifle and Light Infantry Tactics* while serving as commandant of cadets at West Point in 1856. After Hardee took over ownership of the home, Anna continued to live there, often caring for Hardee's children during his absence. Legend says that Confederate spies operated out of the home during the Civil War. Anna Dummett was a loyal Confederate to the end, helping to form the Ladies Memorial Association in 1866 and becoming instrumental in raising funds for the Confederate Memorial (see above). Her name continues to be associated with the city and the Civil War through the United Daughters of the Confederacy Anna Dummett Chapter.

Directions—Continue across, turning left on St. Francis Street until reaching the

Fernandez-Llambias House

31 St. Francis Street
N29°53.273 W081°18.609

The Fernandez-Llambias House dates to before the British rule of 1763, when the home was a single-story dwelling owned by Pedro Fernandez.

The Llambias House was home to three young men who served in the Confederate army; two would die in service. During the war, the family was forced from the city when they would not take the oath of allegiance. In their absence, the house was vandalized. *Courtesy the author.*

When the Spanish regained control of Florida, the home was owned by a Minorcan family who stayed after the change in rulers. In 1838, the second story was added to the house. In 1854, the home was purchased by the Llambias family, who held title for over sixty-five years. The home was purchased in trust by the Carnegie Institution and presented to the St. Augustine Historical Society, which ultimately restored the property. The Altrusa Club is now custodian of the property.

The Llambias family contributed heavily to the Confederate cause during the war. Three sons (Michael George, Joseph Francis and John) all saw action in the war, with only one surviving (see Appendix III). In addition, when the patriarch of the family, Joseph, refused to take an oath of allegiance, he was imprisoned at Fort Marion on the orders of Provost Marshal O.T. Beard. Eventually, Joseph and the rest of his family were sent to Confederate lines on the steamer *Boston*, which left them at Fernandina. After the war, when the remaining family members returned, they found their home vandalized, including the fact that the ground floor had apparently been used as a stable.

Directions—Continue east and cross back over St. Francis Street and continue through Charlotte Street, arriving at

Tovar House

18 St. Francis Street
N29°53.276 W081°18.609

While the original date of construction is unknown, the house is believed to date from before 1763. The house is currently owned by the St. Augustine Historical Society and is part of its "Oldest House" museum complex.

The Tovar House was for many years home to Union general Martin D. Hardin. Hardin appears to have first leased the home in 1885 from owner Francis M. von Balsam for a period of ten years, later renewing the lease in 1893 to start in 1895. This lease included the option to buy the property. In 1912, the property was sold by Louis R. Hite, von Balsam's only heir, to the South Beach Alligator Farm and Museum of Marine Curiosities, Inc. The property was transferred to the St. Augustine Historical Society in 1918, and it has owned the property since.

Directions—Continue east on St. Francis Street until you reach Marine Street. Cross St. Francis Street and you will have reached

St. Francis Barracks

82 Marine Street
N29°53.263 W081°18.571
www.floridaguard.army.mil

What now stands as the St. Francis Barracks is a rebuilt assortment of buildings after fire destroyed all but the coquina walls in 1915. Barracks on this location have been used as military housing by English, Spanish, Confederate and Union troops. In 1921, the property was turned over to the State of Florida and serves as the headquarters for the Florida National Guard.

Be sure to read the several descriptive plaques that line Marine Street.

Directions—Continue south along Marine Street, and on the right-hand side you will arrive at

St. Augustine National Cemetery

104 Marine Street
N29°53.176 W081°18.568
www.cem.va.gov/cems/nchp/staugustine.asp

When arriving at St. Augustine National Cemetery, it will be natural for your eyes to be drawn to the three large pyramids that mark the final resting spot for over 1,400 men who were killed during the Indian Wars in Florida from 1835 to 1842. These monuments to Major Francis L. Dade, his more than 100 troops and others who died during these wars were dedicated on August 14, 1842. Located with the pyramids is a coquina and marble obelisk to commemorate Major Dade and his troops. This marker, erected in 1881, was paid for by troops stationed at St. Francis Barracks. Each man contributed one day of pay toward the funding.

The cemetery was not designated a National Cemetery until the mid-1880s at the request of Quartermaster General Montgomery Meigs. Meigs is perhaps best known for his role in establishing Arlington National Cemetery at the former home of Confederate general Robert E. Lee. Meigs also stood guard at the front door of the Peterson House in Washington, D.C., while President Lincoln lay there on his deathbed.

In 1912 and 1913, additional lands were acquired, bringing the cemetery to its current size of just over 1.3 acres. In 1938, a new superintendent's lodge was added to the property. The cemetery is currently closed to new burials.

The most famous Civil War–related burial is General Martin D. Hardin. Look for the large marble cross that is located near the Dade pyramids and obelisk. Hardin spent many of his post-military years in St. Augustine (see Tovar House, the General's House and also Mission of Nombre de Dios Cemetery above and below).

Another notable Civil War burial is John D. Shellenberger (in some records spelled Shellenbarger). Shellenberger attained the rank of captain serving in Company E of the Sixty-fourth Ohio Infantry. He authored two books dealing with the war after his muster

Top: Erected in 1842, the three pyramids cover vaults containing the remains of 1,468 soldiers who died during the Indian Wars in Florida. The pyramids are commonly called the Dade Monuments in honor of Major Francis L. Dade, whose troops were virtually wiped out during an ambush in 1835. Original photo by George Barker. *Courtesy Library of Congress.*

Right: Headstone for Martin D. and Amelia Hardin located in St. Augustine National Cemetery. *Courtesy the author.*

out. Both deal with comments made by General John Schofield regarding battles at Spring Hill and Franklin.

Shellenberger and his family moved frequently, with census records showing them having lived in Wisconsin, California, Virginia and Florida. In Virginia, he served as superintendent at Hampton National Cemetery and later as superintendent at this cemetery, where he was buried. He and his wife share a large joint stone in section B, numbers 548 and 549.

As you wander through the cemetery, you will also notice many markers for members of the United States Colored Troops. Many of these men were from the Thirty-third USCT, also known as the First South Carolina. This regiment was formed with many former slaves from this area of Florida.

Directions—After your visit to the cemetery, you may wish to walk along the beautiful Matanzas River as you make your way back toward the busier part of town. If you choose to follow the river, you will make your way back toward the Plaza and eventually Fort Marion/Castillo de San Marcos.

Assorted Locations

Following are various locations in and around St. Augustine that those interested in the Civil War might consider visiting. They are off the path from the walking tours above, though several can be reached by foot.

Last Slave Cabin in St. Augustine

94 South Street
N29°52.957 W081°18.765

Located on private property in the Lincolnville historic district sits a small, unassuming building set at the back of a house; to some, it is known as the last slave cabin in St. Augustine. This claim is not without dispute, however, as historians are unable to agree on the former function of a building that is now used for storage. The building is shown on 1830s maps as being on plantation land owned by the Leonardi family and known as Buena Esperanza (Spanish for good hope). The Historic St. Augustine Preservation Board, however, did not find evidence of people having lived in the building during an archaeological dig that took place in the mid-1990s. Historian

This now enlarged building is considered by many historians and archaeologists to be the last remaining slave cabin in St. Augustine. *Courtesy the author.*

David Nolan contends that the trash pits for the building would likely be located under what is now Blanco Street and that until this area is excavated more thoroughly, a definitive answer cannot be given.

The house itself has historic significance other than the outbuilding. Owners Hattie Lee (who passed away in 2011) and James White, along with their family, played a significant role in the struggle for racial equality in St. Augustine during the 1960s, both of them having participated in various demonstrations. Their son Samuel was a member of the St. Augustine Four, a group of young men arrested and made to serve six months in jail and reform school for participating in a sit-in at the Woolworth's lunch counter. Their other children also participated, working to integrate churches, schools and other public facilities. There is a marker in front of the home marking it as part of the Accord Freedom Trail.

The slave cabin is best seen from Blanco Street, where there is a historical marker outlining the history of the building. Please remember that the slave cabin is on private property. Do not attempt to get a closer look without the permission of the owner.

The Generals House

20 Valencia Street
N29°53.491 W081°18.694

The building that now houses the Flagler College Business Services offices sometimes goes by the moniker the Generals House. This is because two different Union generals called this building home after the war. Both John M. Schofield and Martin D. Hardin lived and died at 20 Valencia Street.

General Schofield first occupied the house in 1899 after having spent several previous winters at other locations in the city. It was here that Schofield lived out the last seven years of his life. During this time, he was a prominent fixture on the social circuit. In 1904, the Schofields had the home enlarged by adding a brick wing on the west side. In addition, between 1899 and 1904, a now demolished octagonal structure was added in the backyard. General Schofield passed away in the Generals House in 1906 at the age of

The Generals House served as a home to both John M. Schofield and Martin D. Hardin. The building is now owned by Flagler College. *Courtesy Flagler College Library.*

seventy-four. General Schofield was buried in Arlington National Cemetery in Arlington, Virginia. He is buried in section two, grave 1108.

General Hardin was a resident of the home from 1916 until his death in 1923. Hardin and his second wife, Amelia McLaughlin, came to St. Augustine in 1893, originally living in the Tovar House (see tour two). After General Hardin passed away in 1923, his widow continued to live in the home until her death in 1939. As a memorial to General Hardin, Amelia was a major contributor to the restoration of the La Leche Shrine (see below). General and Mrs. Hardin are buried in the St. Augustine National Cemetery (see tour two).

The Generals House was purchased by Flagler College in the 1970s. With the growing need for administrative offices and building deterioration in mind, the decision was made to undertake a restoration project with an anticipated budget of around $300,000. Interior damage was worse than originally estimated, and the final budget came in at just under $475,000 when the project was completed in 1987. While some of the original structure has been retained, such as staircases and fireplaces, the building was adapted to modern usage. The Florida Trust for Historic Preservation awarded Flagler College its Florida Trust Award for Merit for the Adaptive Use of a Historic Structure in 1988 for the work done.

Villa Zorayda

83 King Street
www.villazorayda.com

The grand Moorish building Villa Zorayda is now a prominent tourist attraction located on busy King Street near Flagler College. Originally built in 1883 using a newly developed poured coquina concrete mixture, it was first used as a winter residence by Franklin W. Smith and his wife, Laura. Smith named the home Villa Zorayda after the second of the three princesses from the Washington Irving novel *The Alhambra*.

The building was such a success that Henry Flagler offered to buy it from Smith. Smith declined but did show Flagler the method of poured coquina concrete that was later used in building the Hotel Ponce de Leon, the Alcazar Hotel, the Memorial Presbyterian Church and also the Grace Methodist Church.

While the building itself has no Civil War ties, the builder, Franklin W. Smith, does. Smith has direct ties with Abraham Lincoln. Smith and his brother Benjamin were arrested upon orders of the secretary of the navy without warning on June 17, 1864, and ultimately charged with "fraud upon the United States." After a trial of 115 days, the expected guilty verdict was reached. Smith had an ally in Charles Sumner, who worked late into the night to prove to President Lincoln that a great injustice had been done to the Smith brothers. Lincoln declared the verdict null and demanded that the accused be released. After news of the tragic assassination of Abraham Lincoln, Franklin W. Smith was given the honor of leading the gathering at the Tremont Temple Baptist Church in Boston.

The Tremont Temple itself has several associations with Lincoln and the Civil War. In 1848, while on a political tour stumping for Zachary Taylor, Lincoln heard former New York governor and future secretary of state William Seward give an antislavery speech there and is alleged to have told Seward that the slavery question would need more attention than it had been given. In addition, the Temple was the first location in Boston where the Emancipation Proclamation was read in 1863.

Markland (Anderson House)

102 King Street
N29°53.532 W081°19.032 (coordinates based on street parking)

The large, imposing white house that is set back from King Street is the former Anderson House and is now owned by Flagler College, which uses it for offices and occasional entertaining.

Andrew Anderson Sr. began the construction of Markland in 1839, with the majority of the building completed by 1843 under the direction of his widow, Clarissa. Clarissa was a staunch Union supporter during the war, and numerous gatherings were held at Markland during the Union occupation of the city. The orange groves surrounding Markland were legendary, and many soldiers wrote home about them.

Andrew Anderson Jr. briefly served in the Third Florida Infantry Company B (St. Augustine Blues) before hiring a substitute, S. Benet, and leaving the state to study medicine in New York. It appears he made only a brief visit home during the war but afterward returned to his native city for good. His legacy lives on in the statue of Ponce de Leon and also the two famous lions that sit at the western end of the Bridge of Lions, which he generously donated to the city.

Mission of Nombre de Dios

27 Ocean Avenue
www.missionandshrine.org
www.ssjfl.org

Home of the famous 208-foot-tall stainless-steel cross, Nombre de Dios is really a lot more than that single cross. Located on the well-manicured grounds are a church, chapels, a cemetery, archaeological work and a gift shop. If you drive here, I suggest parking near the gift shop. Here you will find everything imaginable for the Catholic faith; there are also restrooms and water fountains. This is also a good starting point for walking the grounds. Our tour will involve the cemetery area, but I highly recommend a walk around the rest of the grounds.

A beautiful vine-covered chapel known as Our Lady of La Leche Shrine has a long history dating back to 1615. The building now standing is the fourth at this location, with construction having begun in 1918. Much of the restoration funding came from the widow of Union general Martin Hardin, and two plaques on the outside of the shrine note the Hardins' participation.

Our Lady of La Leche Shrine, which is located on the property of the Mission of Nombre de Dios, was restored by Martin Hardin's widow in his honor. *Courtesy the author.*

On the main descriptive plaque to the left of the entry are the words "Restored and furnished as a chapel by Mrs. General Hardin in memory of General Martin D. Hardin in 1925." The plaque on the right-hand side of the entry reads, "In Memoriam General M.D. Hardin 'I have loved O Lord the beauty of thy house and the place where thy glory dwelleth.'"

Though freed after the war, it was evident that the former slaves would be in some ways reliant on white people to help them move into their new role. Education for both children and adults was needed. To help fill this need, Bishop Augustin Verot requested help from the Sisters of St. Joseph in Le Puy, France. The sisters responded enthusiastically, sending an original group of eight and then later adding to this number. The sisters worked tirelessly in both St. Augustine and Savannah, Georgia, to carry out their mission. The Sisters of St. Joseph are still an active congregation today, continuing to carry out the mission they started almost 150 years ago.

Inside a large, low walled area are the grave sites of six members of the Sisters of St. Joseph. Each grave is marked with a cross, and the area has a wooden informational marker.

Frederick Douglass Speech Site

St. George Street near Treasury Street on the left-hand side when walking toward the Plaza
N29°53.638 W081°18.772

During August 1889, Frederick Douglass was scheduled to give a speech at the Sub-Tropical Exhibition that was taking place in Jacksonville. Despite

A street marker notes the location of the building where Frederick Douglass delivered a speech in 1889. *Courtesy the author.*

limited time, Douglass was convinced to take a train ride to St. Augustine, where he was given an afternoon reception at the second-story Genovar Opera House. The approximately seven hundred people in attendance, both black and white, eagerly waited for Douglass to speak. Not having expected to visit St. Augustine, he delivered a portion of his Jacksonville speech before time constraints forced him to leave.

The Genovar Opera House and other associated buildings burned to the ground in April 1914. In June 2009, the City of St. Augustine erected a small marker commemorating Douglass's trip to the city.

Appendix I

Ordinance of Secession

We, the people of the State of Florida in Convention assembled, do solemnly ordain, publish and declare: That the State of Florida hereby withdraws herself from the Confederacy of States existing under the name of the United States of America, and from the existing Government of said States: and that all political connection between her and the Government of said States ought to be and the same is hereby totally annulled, and said union of States dissolved: and the State of Florida is hereby declared Sovereign and Independent Nation: and that all ordinances heretofore adopted in so far as they create or recognize said Union, are rescinded: and all laws or parts of laws in force in this State, in so far as they recognize or assent to said Union be and they are hereby repealed
Done in open Convention, January 10th, A.D. 1861

John C. McGehee President			John Beard
A.W. Nicholson	S.J. Baker	Jackson Morton	Abraham Kyrkyndale Allison
A.J.T. Wright	S.B. Stephens	E.E. Simpson	Danl Ladd
R.D. Jordan	Freeman B. Irwin	David Lewis	James Kirksey
Adam McNealy	McQueen McIntosh	Thompson B. Lamar	G.W. Parkhill

Thomas Y. Henry	Saml W. Spencer	J. Patton Anderson	Geo. T. Ward
E.C. Love	D.D. McLean	Thomas M. Palmer	W.G.M. Davis
A.J. Lea	Lewis A. Folsom	William S. Dilworth	Joseph Thomas
W.H. Sever	Green H. Hunter	J.M. Daniel	Mathew Solana
E.P. Barronton	Jas. A. Newman	T.J. Hendrick	Jas. O. Devall
Joseph Finegan	Arthur J.T. Wright	J.P. Sanderson	R.G. Mays
James G. Cooper	Isaac S. Coon	Jas. B. Owens	John C. Pelot
Jas. H. Chandler	John J. Lamb	Summerfield M.G. Gary	James B. Dawkins
David G. Leigh	Isaac N. Rutland	W. McGahagin	William W. Woodruff
James Gettis	Wm. Pinkney	Asa F. Tift	W.B. Yates
S.S. Alderman	Winer Bethel	James L.G. Baker	John Morrison
Alexander L. McCaskill	Joseph A. Collier of Jacksonville		
Attest William S. Harris, Secretary			

Appendix II

St. Augustine Blues

Third Florida Infantry Company B

Officers

John Lott Phillips Sr.—Captain
Laurence M. Andrew—First Lieutenant
Charles L. Ridgely—Second Lieutenant
Irvine Drysdale—Third Lieutenant
Fatio Dunham—First Sergeant
John A. Rose—Second Sergeant
Edward S. Hernandez—Third Sergeant
Bartolo D. Ponce—Fourth Sergeant
Phillip Leonardy—First Corporal
Joseph E. Masters—Second Corporal
Joseph Leonardy—Third Corporal
Christobal M. Bravo—Fourth Corporal

PRIVATES

James W. Allen	Andrew Anderson	Andrew Anderson	Emanuel P. Andrew
Francis P. Andrew	Joseph P. Andrew	Laboris B. Andrew	Nicholas Andrew
Francis C. Arnan	Alexander Avice	Andrew J. Beggs	Stephen A. Benet
Henry Bridier	Louis D. Bridier	Theodore F. Bridier	Charles H. Brush
Edward Clifford Brush	Henry Bryan	Robert C. Burritt	Andrew P. Canova
Antonio L. Canova	Joseph Capo	Philip V. Capo	Stephen Carreras
George A. Colee	William Colee	Samuel S. Cook	James Crosby
Henry C. Dunham	Oregon Dunham	Joseph B. Ferreira	Tony Fontaine
Charles Foster	John Funte	Bartolo Genovar	William Genovar
Francis H.R. Gould	James M. Gould	Charles F. Haddock	George Willets Hanford
Raphael Hemanes	Joseph V. Hernandez	Edgard W. Hunter	General Jackson Hussey
Joseph Irwin	Ramon L. Irwin	Hilliard Lee	Celestial John Leonardy
John Leonardy	Antonio Llambias	John Llambias	Alonzo Lopez
Emanuel M. Lopez	John Manucy	Decidario S. Masters	Paul Edward Masters
Peter B. Masters	Peter C. Masters	Theodosia B. Masters	Daniel J. Mickler
David A. Middleton	William C. Middleton	James A. Miller	James J. Miller
John Miller	William Miranda	Henry H. Neligan	Michael Neligan
Emanuel Osborn	William E. Osteen	Bartolo J. Pacetti	Herbert Alexander Pacetti
Joseph A. Pacetti	Isaac Papino	Edward Ambrose Papy	Isadore B. Papy
John Papy	John Lott Phillips Jr.	Paul Geiger Phillips	William Pomar
Anthony Ponce	Isadora B. Ponce	James B. Ponce	Thomas Ponce

Benjamin Powers	Frank W. Sams	James P. Sanchez	Celestina H. Segui
Charles Downing Segui	Joseph M. Solana	James A. Spear	Joseph Spencer
John A. Steinbeck	John M. Stephens	Thomas Turner	Domingo B. Usina
Michael Usina	Michael Sanchez Usina	Richard W. Voss	Francis Marion Weems
Tony Wetters	John A. Whitby	Daniel T. Wickwire	John W. Willard
William W. Williams	George W. Winn	Raphael F. Ximanies	

Appendix III

St. Augustine Confederates Who Died During the War*

Joseph Andreu	Francis Baya	Casimero Benet	Louis Bridier
Henry Bryan	Samuel Buffington	Mariano Capella	Gaspar Carreras
R. Francis Dancy	Henry G. Dunham	Abraham DuPont	William DuPont
Andrew Floyd	Philip Gomez	Archibald Gould	James Hanson
William J. Hardee	Edward C. Humphreys	James Hurlbert	Jose Irwin
John M. Llambias	Michael G. Llambias	Alfonso Lopez	Antonio Lopez
Peter Masters	Antonio Mickler	George Mickler	Jacob Mickler
Joseph Noda	Eusebio Pacetti	Edward A. Papy	Frank Papy
Marine Papy	Bartolo Pinkham	John Ponce	Thomas Ponce
Nathaniel Powers	Felix Rante	R. Jenckes Reid	Richard Russell
John Stevens	Henaro Triay	James Walton	Frank Weems
J. Wescott Willard			

**Names are posted on the Confederate Memorial located in the Plaza de la Constitucion*

NOTES

CHAPTER 1

1. Mrs. Frances Smith to Edmund Kirby Smith, January 11, 1860, quoted in Parks, *General Edmund Kirby Smith*, 104.
2. Greenleaf, "History of the Confederate Monument," 6–7.
3. Wooster, "Florida Secession Convention," 374.
4. Johns, *Florida During the Civil War*, 1–13.
5. Graham, *Awakening of St. Augustine*, 88.
6. Wooster, "Florida Secession Convention," 374–75.
7. Dodd, "Edmund Ruffin's Account," 70.
8. Wooster, "Florida Secession Convention," 376–78.

CHAPTER 2

9. *St. Augustine Examiner*, November 24, 1860, and December 29, 1860.
10. *Official Records of the Union and Confederate Armies*, ser. 1, vol. 1, 333. (Hereafter cited as *ORA*. All further references are to ser. 1 unless otherwise noted.)
11. Fretwell, *Civil War Times*, 21; Mrs. Frances Smith to Edmund Kirby Smith, January 11, 1860, quoted in Parks, *General Edmund Kirby Smith.*
12. Fretwell, *Civil War Times*, 2–3.
13. Harvey, *Daring Daughters*, 28–31.

14. Fretwell, *Civil War Times*, 2–3; *Official Records of the Union and Confederate Navies*, vol. 12, 207–8. (Hereafter cited as *ORN*).
15. Staudenraus, "War Correspondent's View," 60.
16. Fretwell, *Civil War Times*, 23–24.
17. *ORA*, vol. 6, 406.
18. Sweett, *New Smyrna*, 1–8.
19. *ORN*, vol. 12, 595–97.
20. For information regarding Christobal (Christoval) Bravo, please see his compiled service report. Included is discharge paperwork citing "vascular disease of the heart."
21. Quoted in Parks, *General Edmund Kirby Smith*, 123. No notation is provided as to the date of her letter to her son, Edmund.
22. *ORN*, vol. 12, 595–97.
23. Quoted in Graham, *Awakening of St. Augustine*, 103.
24. Biographical information on Louis Bell may be found at www.library.unh.edu/special/index.php/louis-bell.
25. All above Louis Bell quotations taken from Louis Bell to Wife, March 26, 1862, Louis Bell Papers, Milne Special Collections and Archives at University of New Hampshire, Durham, NH. See also *ORA*, vol. 14, 333–34.
26. Louis Bell to Wife, March 26, 1862; *ORA*, vol. 14, 356–57, and quoted in Graham, *Awakening of St. Augustine*, 108–9.
27. Bryant, *Diary of Elias A. Bryant*, 56.
28. Leander Harris to Emmy, April 17, 1862, Leander Harris Letters, Milne Special Collections and Archives at University of New Hampshire, Durham, NH.
29. Leander Harris to My Darling Wife, April 13, 1862.
30. Leander Harris to Emmy, June 8, 1862.
31. Henry Haskell Diary, July 4, 1862, State Library and Archives of Florida, Tallahassee, FL.
32. Bryant, *Diary of Elias A. Bryant*, 64–65; Leander Harris to Emmy, June 8, 1862; Henry Haskell Diary, June 13, 1862.
33. Graham, *Awakening of St. Augustine*, 103–4.
34. Biographical information on Haldimand S. Putnam may be found at scholar.library.miami.edu/shedd/letters/putnam.html.
35. William H. Haskell Diary, September 6, 1862, State Library and Archives of Florida, Tallahassee, FL.
36. Graham, *Awakening of St. Augustine*, 114–16; *St. Augustine Record*, "Recollections of Sanchez," April 30, 1912.

37. Calvin Shedd to Wife & Children, October 10 and 12, 1862, Calvin Shedd Papers, University of Miami, Miami, FL.
38. Personal Reflections of Service in the Civil War written by Ferdinand Davis, 12–13, Raymond Cazallis Davis Papers, University of Michigan, Bentley Historical Library, Ann Arbor, MI.
39. Calvin Shedd to Wife, March 14, 1863.
40. Little, *Seventh Regiment New Hampshire*, 85–86.
41. Calvin Shedd to Ones at Home, Thanksgiving Eve, 1862.
42. Little, *Seventh Regiment New Hampshire*, 88.
43. Ibid., 89; *ORA*, vol. 14, 224.
44. Ibid., 96.
45. Walkley, *History of the Seventh Connecticut*, 68.
46. Palmer, *History of the Forty-eighth Regiment*, 129; Nichols, *Perry's Saints*, 180–81; *ORA*, vol. 28, part 2, 42–43.
47. Oliver Walker to Father & Mother, November 22, 1863, Pearce Museum at Navarro College, Corsicana, TX.
48. Graham, *Awakening of St. Augustine*, 126–27; Lieutenant James H. Linsley Diary, December 30, 1863, George A. Smathers Libraries at University of Florida, Gainesville, FL.
49. Lieutenant James H. Linsley Diary, November 6, 1863; William Norton Diary, November 2, 1863, Connecticut Historical Society, Hartford, CT; John Burnett to Friend, November 16, 1863, Connecticut Historical Society, Hartford, CT.
50. Lieutenant James H. Linsley Diary, November 26, 1863, and William Norton Diary, November 29, 1863.
51. Lieutenant James H. Linsley Diary, January 1, 1864.
52. Trumbull, *Sermon Preached to the Tenth Connecticut*, 13–17.
53. William Norton Diary, April 15, 1864.
54. Albert W. Peck, Civil War Reminiscences, 43–45, State Library and Archives of Florida, Tallahassee, FL.
55. Marcus, *New Canaan Private*, 84–85.
56. Peck, Civil War Reminiscences, 48–49; Marcus, *New Canaan Private*, 88–89.
57. Peck, Civil War Reminiscences, 54; Marcus, *New Canaan Private*, 99–102.
58. Graham, *Awakening of St. Augustine*, 134–35.
59. Ibid., 136–41.

CHAPTER 3

60. Robinson, *Confederate Privateers*, 59–62.
61. *St. Augustine News*, October 1, 1841.
62. *Ancient City*, April 17, 1852, and July 10, 1852.
63. Robinson, *Confederate Privateers*, 62–63.
64. Biographical information regarding William Baya may be found in the Baya file, St. Augustine Historical Society Research Library.
65. *New York Herald*, July 22, 1861.
66. Robinson, *Confederate Privateers*, 79–88.
67. Norman Brownson to Henry Summer, August 6, 1861, Henry Summer Letters, Southern Historical Collection, Chapel Hill, NC.
68. Biographical information regarding J.F. Carlsen may be found at www.hunley.org/main_index.asp?content=CARLSEN.
69. *Charleston Mercury*, August 26, 1861.

CHAPTER 4

70. Reiger, "Secession of Florida," 358–68.
71. John F. Whitney Family Record, 59, Whitney File, St. Augustine Historical Society Research Library.
72. *New York Times*, April 20, 1902; Boren, "John F. Whitney."
73. French adjective meaning proper or correct.
74. The Ocklawaha River joins the St. Johns River near the city of Palatka. The name is an adaption of the Creek Indian word *ak-lowahy*, meaning muddy.
75. Emerson, *Mary Lincoln's Insanity Case*, 6–7.
76. Taliaferro, *All the Great Prizes*, 65–82.
77. May, "Ulysses S. Grant's Visit," 1–2.
78. Ibid., 4–9.
79. Quoted in May, "Ulysses S. Grant's Visit," 15.
80. May, "Ulysses S. Grant's Visit," 23.
81. Ibid., 21–22.
82. *Frank Leslie's Illustrated Newspaper*, March 3, 1861.
83. Abraham Lincoln, March 18, 1865, Abraham Lincoln Papers, Series 1, General Correspondence, Library of Congress, Washington, D.C.
84. *Boston Globe*, November 18, 2012.
85. Franklin W. Smith, Last Will and Testament April 12, 1906, Franklin W. Smith File, St. Augustine Historical Society Research Library.

86. *East Florida Gazette* 15 (July 1995).
87. Oliver, "Franklin W. Smith."
88. Colburn, *Racial Change*, 19.
89. Undated newspaper clipping, Amusements File, St. Augustine Historical Society Research Library. The Lincolnville Theatre is shown in the 1916 St. Augustine City Directory as being located at 92 Washington Street, and J.M. Harmon is shown as the proprietor.

Chapter 5

90. Data and statistics were compiled from the 1850 and 1860 United States Federal Census Reports.
91. Meyer, "Venancio Sanchez," 17–18.
92. *Newport Mercury*, January 23, 1926; United States Federal Census Records 1880, 1910, 1920; Freedman's Bank Records, 1865–1871.
93. Bloomfield, *Bloomfield's Illustrated Historical Guide*, 30–31.
94. Hardy, *Down South*, 171–72.
95. Nichols, *Perry's Saints*, 181; Bryant, *Diary of Elias A. Bryant*, 54.
96. *St. Augustine Evening Record*, July 15, 1914.
97. *St. Augustine Record*, September 27, 2009.
98. Quoted in Amy Howard, "Public Market (Slave Market)," on augustine.com/history/black_history/slavemarket.
99. Rose, *Beloved Strangers*, 90.
100. *St. Augustine Record*, February 21, 2004.
101. Quoted in Colburn and Landers, *African American Heritage*, 164.
102. *St. Augustine Record*, February 21, 2004.
103. Roe, *Twenty-fourth Regiment Massachusetts*, 251–52.
104. Hartman and Coles, *Biographical Rosters*.
105. *St. Augustine Record*, March 7, 2011.
106. *Evening Telegram*, February 13, 1894.
107. *St. Augustine Record*, March 7, 2011.

Chapter 6

108. Biographical information on Stephen V. Benet may be found at www.drbronsontours.com/bronsonhistorypagestaugustinecivlwarpage2.html.
109. Gray, "Edmund J. Davis."

110. Strickland, "Dummett Family Saga," 3–9.
111. Quoted in Hughes, *General William J. Hardee*, 88.
112. Ibid., 97.
113. Ibid., 312–13.
114. Reuben H. Walworth to Abraham Lincoln, November 18, 1861, Abraham Lincoln Papers, Library of Congress, Washington, D.C.
115. Warner, *Generals in Blue*, 205–6.
116. *St. Augustine News*, January 25, 1891; *Florida Times Union*, February 6, 1892.
117. *Tatler*, February 20, 1892.
118. Ibid., March, 26, 1892.
119. Ibid., March 5, 1892.
120. Ibid., January 18, 1908.
121. *St. Augustine Record*, December 13, 1923.
122. *St. Augustine Evening Record*, May 1, 1924.
123. Wessels, *Born to Be a Soldier*, 2–4.
124. Quoted in Ibid., 18.
125. Quoted in Ibid., 51.
126. Ibid., 65.
127. Ibid., 85.
128. *New York Times*, December 31, 1886; *Florida Times Union*, March 19, 1887; *East Florida Gazette* 26 (Spring 2008).
129. Warner, *Generals in Blue*, 425–26.
130. *Tatler*, January 16, 1897.
131. Ibid., April 7, 1900; *St. Augustine Evening Record*, August 31, 1901.
132. *St. Augustine Evening Record*, March 5, 1906.
133. Parks, *General Edmund Kirby Smith*, 6–36.
134. Quoted in Ibid., 479–80.
135. *New York Times*, March 29, 1893.
136. "Statue of General E. Kirby Smith," 166–67.

Bibliography

Articles

Bittle, George C. "Florida Prepares for War, 1860–1861." *Florida Historical Quarterly* 51 (October 1972): 143–52.

Boren, Courtney. "John F. Whitney & Spengler Island." *St. Augustine Archaeological Association Newsletter* 25 (October 2010): 1–6.

Coles, David, and Zack C. Waters. "Indian Fighter, Confederate Soldier, Blockade Runner and Scout: The Life and Letters of Jacob E. Mickler." *El Escribano* 34 (1997): 35–69.

"Confederate Privateer *Jefferson Davis*." *The Bayonet SCV Col. Isaac Williams Smith Camp* #458 3 (March 2008): 7.

Dahl, Curtis. "Lincoln Saves a Reformer." *American Heritage* 23 (October 1972).

———. "Mr. Smith's American Acropolis." *American Heritage* 7 (June 1956).

Dodd, Dorothy. "Edmund Ruffin's Account of the Florida Secession Convention: A Diary." *Florida Historical Quarterly* 12 (October 1933): 70.

———. "The Secession Movement in Florida, 1850–1861 Part I." *Florida Historical Quarterly* 12 (July 1933): 3–24.

———. "The Secession Movement in Florida, 1850–1861 Part II." *Florida Historical Quarterly* 12 (October 1933): 45–66.

East, Omega G. "St. Augustine During the Civil War." *Florida Historical Quarterly* 31 (October 1952): 75–91.

James, Joseph B. "Edmund Kirby Smith's Boyhood in Florida." *Florida Historical Quarterly* 14 (April 1936): 244–54.

Jones, James P. "Grant Forecasts the Future of Florida." *Florida Historical Quarterly* 39 (July 1960): 52–54.

[L.H.L.?] "Lola Sanchez's Ride: What a Cuban Girl Did for Confederates." *Confederate Veteran* 17 (August 1909): 409–10.

May, Jessica A. "Ulysses S. Grant's Visit to St. Augustine." *El Escribano* 46 (2009): 1–30.

Oliver, Elizabeth Kimball. "A Bostonian and His Moorish Castle." *East Florida Gazette* 15, no. 3 (July 1995): 3.

"The Public Market Place." *El Escribano* 54 (October 1964): 1–2.

Reiger, John F. "Florida after Secession: Abandonment by the Confederacy and Its Consequences." *Florida Historical Quarterly* 50 (October 1971): 128–42.

———. "Secession of Florida from the Union—A Minority Decision?" *Florida Historical Quarterly* 46 (April 1968): 358–68.

Ruffin, Edmund. "Account of the Florida Secession Convention: A Diary." *Florida Historical Quarterly* 12 (October 1933): 67–76.

"Statue of General E. Kirby Smith." *Confederate Veteran* 30 (May 1922): 166–67.

Staudenraus, P.J., ed. "A War Correspondent's View of St. Augustine and Fernandina: 1863." *Florida Historical Quarterly* 41 (July 1962): 60–65.

Strickland, Alice. "The Dummett Family Saga." *Journal of the Halifax Historical Society* 2, no. 1 (1956): 3–13.

Tonyan, Rick. "The Last Confederate General: St. Augustine's Edmund Kirby Smith." *Halifax Magazine* (May 1999).

"Two Days in April, 1865." *East Florida Gazette* 10, no. 1 (July 1987): 4.

Van Gordon, John H. "Captain Coxetter and the *Jefferson Davis*." *El Escribano* 43 (April 1962): 4–8.

Waterbury, Jean Parker. "The Many Lives of the Llambias House." *El Escribano* 34 (1997): 5–35.

———. "The Treasurer's House." *El Escribano* 31 (1994): 1–240.

Wooster, Ralph A. "The Florida Secession Convention." *Florida Historical Quarterly* 36 (April 1958): 373–85.

BOOKS

Amory, Charles Bean. *A Brief Record of the Army Life of Charles B. Amory*. N.p.: privately published, 1902.

Bloomfield, Max. *Bloomfield's Illustrated Historical Guide, Embracing an Account of the Antiquities of St. Augustine (with map) to Which Is Added a Condensed Guide of the St. John's, Ocklawaha, Halifax, and Indian Rivers*. St. Augustine, FL: Max Bloomfield, Bookseller, Newsdealer & Stationer, 1884.

Bryant, Elias A. *The Diary of Elias A. Bryant of Francestown, N.H. As Written by Him While in His More Than Three Years Service in the U.S. Army in the Civil War*. Concord, NH: Rumford Press, n.d.

Clark, James C. *Presidents in Florida: How the Presidents Have Shaped Florida and How Florida Has Influenced the Presidents*. Sarasota, FL: Pineapple Press, 2012.

Colburn, David R. *Racial Change & Community Crisis: St. Augustine, Florida, 1877–1980*. Gainesville: University Press of Florida, 1991.

Colburn, David R., and Jane L. Landers, eds. *The African American Heritage of Florida*. Gainesville: University Press of Florida, 1995.

Dickison, Mary Elizabeth. *Dickison and His Men: Reminiscences of the War in Florida 1890*. Facsimile ed. Jacksonville, FL: San Marco Bookstore, 1984.

Emerson, Jason. *The Madness of Mary Lincoln*. Carbondale: Southern Illinois University Press, 2007.

———. *Mary Lincoln's Insanity Case: A Documentary History*. Urbana: University of Illinois Press, 2012.

Fairbanks, George R. *The Spaniards of Florida, Jacksonville*. 1868. Facsimile edition with new material added by Donald D. Spencer, Ormond Beach, FL: Camelot Publishing Company, 2003.

Fretwell, Jacqueline K., ed. *Civil War Times in St. Augustine*. Port Salerno: Florida Classics Library, 1988.

Gannon, Michael, ed. *The New History of Florida*. Gainesville: University Press of Florida, 1996.

———. *Rebel Bishop: Augustin Verot: Florida's Civil War Prelate*. Gainesville: University Press of Florida, 1997.

Gaske, Frederick P. *Florida Civil War Heritage Trail*. Tallahassee: Florida Association of Museums, n.d.

Graham, Thomas. *The Awakening of St. Augustine: The Anderson Family and the Oldest City: 1821–1924*. St. Augustine, FL: St. Augustine Historical Society, 1978.

Griffin, Patricia C. *Ralph Waldo Emerson in St. Augustine*. St. Augustine, FL: St. Augustine Historical Society, 1995.

Hardy, Lady Mary Anne Duffus. *Down South*. London: Chapman and Hall, Ltd., 1883.

Hartman, David, and David Coles. *Biographical Rosters of Florida's Confederate and Union Troops, 1861–1865*. 6 vols. Wilmington, NC: Broadfoot Publishing Company, 1995.

Harvey, Karen. *America's First City: St. Augustine's Historic Neighborhoods*. Lake Buena Vista, FL: Tailored Tours Publications, 1992.

———. *Daring Daughters: St. Augustine's Feisty Females, 1565–2000*. Virginia Beach, VA: Donning Company, 2002.

———. *St. Augustine and St. Johns County: A Pictorial History*. Norfolk, VA: Donning Company, 1980.

Hughes, Nathaniel Cheairs, Jr. *General William J. Hardee: Old Reliable*. Baton Rouge: Louisiana State University Press, 1965.

Johns, John E. *Florida During the Civil War.* Gainesville: University of Florida Press, 1963.

Johnson, James Weldon. *Along This Way*. 1933. Facsimile edition, New York: Da Capo Press, 1973.

Little, Henry. *The Seventh Regiment New Hampshire Volunteers in the War of the Rebellion*. Concord: Seventh New Hampshire Veteran Association, 1896.

Loring, William Wing. *A Confederate Soldier in Egypt*. New York: Dodd, Mead, and Company, 1884.

Manucy, Albert, ed. *The History of Castillo de San Marcos & Fort Matanzas: From Contemporary Narratives and Letters*. Washington, D.C.: National Park Service Source Book Series Number Three, 1959.

Marcus, Edward, ed. *A New Canaan Private in the Civil War: Letters of Justus M. Silliman, 17th Connecticut Volunteers*. New Canaan, CT: New Canaan Historical Society, 1984.

McCarthy, Kevin M. *African American Sites in Florida*. Sarasota, FL: Pineapple Press, 2007.

McGoldrick, Sister Thomas Joseph. *Beyond the Call: The Legacy of the Sisters of St. Joseph of St. Augustine, Florida*. N.p.: Xlibris, 2008.

Mitchell, Florence S. *Sacred to the Memory: A History of the Huguenot Cemetery 1821–1884, St. Augustine, Florida*. St. Augustine, FL: Friends of the Huguenot Cemetery, 1998.

Nichols, James M. *Perry's Saints or the Fighting Parson's Regiment in the War of the Rebellion*. Boston: D. Lothrop and Company, 1885.

Nolan, David, Jean Ellen Fitzpatrick and Ken Barrett Jr. *The Houses of St. Augustine*. Sarasota, FL: Pineapple Press, 1995.

Palmer, Abraham J. *The History of the Forty-eighth Regiment New York State Volunteers in the War for the Union 1861–1865*. New York: Veteran Association of the Regiment, 1885.

Parks, Joseph H. *General Edmund Kirby Smith C.S.A*. Baton Rouge: Louisiana State University Press, 1982.

Pritchard, Myra Helmer. *The Dark Days of Abraham Lincoln's Widow, as Revealed by Her Own Letters*. Edited by Jason Emerson. Carbondale: Southern Illinois University Press, 2011.

Quinn, Jane. *Minorcans in Florida: Their History and Heritage*. St. Augustine, FL: Mission Press, 1975.

Raab, James W. *W.W. Loring: Florida's Forgotten General*. New York: Sunflower University Press, 1996.

Revels, Tracy J. *Grander in Her Daughters: Florida's Women During the Civil War*. Columbia: University of South Carolina Press, 2004.

Rivers, Larry Eugene. *Slavery in Florida: Territorial Days to Emancipation*. Gainesville: University Press of Florida, 2000.

Robinson, William Morrison, Jr. *The Confederate Privateers*. 1928. Reprint, Columbia: University of South Carolina Press, 1994.

Roe, Alfred S. *The Twenty-fourth Regiment Massachusetts Volunteers 1861–1866 New England Guard Regiment*. Worcester, MA: Twenty-fourth Veteran Association, 1907.

Rose, Anne C. *Beloved Strangers: Interfaith Families in Nineteenth Century America*. Cambridge, MA: Harvard University Press, 2001.

Schafer, Daniel L. *Thunder on the River: The Civil War in Northeast Florida*. Gainesville: University Press of Florida, 2010.

Scharf, J. Thomas. *History of the Confederate States Navy: From Its Organization to the Surrender of Its Last Vessel*. New York: Rogers & Sherwood, 1887.

Sheppard, Jonathan C. *By the Noble Daring of Her Sons: The Florida Brigade of the Army of Tennessee*. Tuscaloosa: University of Alabama Press, 2012.

Shofner, Jerrell H. *Nor Is It Over Yet: Florida in the Era of Reconstruction 1863–1877*. Gainesville: University Press of Florida, 1974.

Silverstone, Paul H. *Warships of the Civil War Navies*. Annapolis, MD: Naval Institute Press, 1989.

Smith, Edmund Kirby. *To Mexico with Scott: Letters of Captain E. Kirby Smith to His Wife*. Edited by Emma Blackwood. Cambridge, MA: Harvard University Press, 1917.

Smith, Franklin W. *The Conspiracy in the U.S. Navy Department against Franklin W. Smith of Boston 1861–1865*. New York: Press of the American Publishing Company, 1890.

Sweett, Zelia W. *New Smyrna, Florida in the Civil War.* New Smyrna Beach, FL: Volusia County Historical Commission, 1963.

Taliaferro, John. *All the Great Prizes: The Life of John Hay, from Lincoln to Roosevelt*. New York: Simon and Schuster, 2013.

Taylor, Paul. *Discovering the Civil War in Florida: A Reader and Guide*. Sarasota, FL: Pineapple Press Inc., 2012.

Taylor, Robert A. *Rebel Storehouse: Florida's Contribution to the Confederacy*. Tuscaloosa: University of Alabama Press, 2003.

Tebeau, Charlton W., and William Marina. *A History of Florida*. Coral Gables, FL: University of Miami Press, 1999.

Trumbull, H. Clay. *Desirableness of Active Service: A Sermon Preached to the Tenth Connecticut Regiment at St. Augustine, FLA., on Sabbath, April 10th, 1864*. Hartford, CT: Press of Case, Lockwood, and Company, 1864.

Van Campen, J.T. *St. Augustine, Florida's Colonial Capital*. St. Augustine, FL: St. Augustine Historical Society, 1959.

Walkley, Stephen. *History of the Seventh Connecticut Volunteer Infantry: Hawley's Brigade, Terry's Division, Tenth Army Corps 1861–1865*. Southington, CT: self-published, 1905.

Warner, Ezra J. *Generals in Blue: Lives of the Union Commanders*. Baton Rouge: Louisiana State University Press, 2006.

———. *Generals in Gray: Lives of the Confederate Commanders*. Baton Rouge: Louisiana State University Press, 2006.

The War of the Rebellion: A Compilation of the Official Records of the Union and Confederate Armies. 128 vols., 3 series. Washington, D.C.: United States Government Printing Office, 1889.

The War of the Rebellion: A Compilation of the Official Records of the Union and Confederate Navies. 31 vols. Washington, D.C.: United States Government Printing Office, 1894–1922.

Waterbury, Jean Parker, ed. *The Oldest City: St. Augustine, Saga of Survival*. St. Augustine, FL: St. Augustine Historical Society, 1983.

———. *The Oldest House*. St. Augustine, FL: St. Augustine Historical Society, 1984.

Waters, Zach C., and James C. Edmonds. *A Small but Spartan Band: The Florida Brigade in Lee's Army of Northern Virginia*. Tuscaloosa: University of Alabama Press, 2010.

Wessels, William L. *Born to Be a Soldier: The Military Career of William Wing Loring of St. Augustine, Florida*. Fort Worth: Texas Christian University Press, 1971.

Wright, J. Leitch, Jr. *British St. Augustine*. St. Augustine, FL: Historic St. Augustine Preservation Board, 1975.

Wynne, Lewis N., and Robert A. Taylor. *Florida in the Civil War*. Charleston, SC: Arcadia Publishing, 2001.

Wynne, Nick, and Joe Crankshaw. *Florida Civil War Blockades: Battling for the Coast*. Charleston, SC: The History Press, 2011.

INTERNET SOURCES

Ancestry, www.ancestry.com
Findagrave, www.findagrave.com
Florida Memory Project, www.floridamemory.com
Fold3, www.fold3.com
History of St. Augustine, drbronsontours.com
St. Augustine Lighthouse, www.staugustinelighthouse.org
United States Census 1850, www.census.gov/prod/www/abs/decennial/1850.html
United States Census 1860, www.census.gov/prod/www/abs/decennial/1860.html

MANUSCRIPTS AND ARCHIVES

Connecticut Historical Society, Hartford, CT
John A. Burnett Letter
Louis Filley Diary
William Norton Diary
Derby Historical Society, Ansonia, CT
Henry C. Williams Diary
Flagler College, St. Augustine, FL
The Generals House File
Library of Congress, Washington, D.C.
Abraham Lincoln Papers
Milne Special Collections and Archives at University of New Hampshire, Durham, New Hampshire
Louis Bell Papers
Leander Harris Letters
Pearce Museum at Navarro College, Corsicana, TX
Oliver Walker Letter
Southern Historical Collection, Chapel Hill, NC
Henry Summer Letters
State Library and Archives of Florida, Tallahassee, FL
Henry Blakeman Papers
Edward Griswold Papers
Henry Haskell Diary
William H. Haskell Diary
Albert W. Peck Civil War Reminiscences
Liberty G. Raymond Papers
Samuel Wolcott Papers

St. Augustine Historical Society Research Library, St. Augustine, FL
Amusements File
Baya File
Coxetter File
Dummett File
Genovar File
Martin Hardin File
Sanchez File
John Schofield File
Justus M. Silliman Papers
Solana File
Whitney File
University of Florida, Gainesville, FL
Lieutenant James H. Linsley Diary
David Levy Yulee Papers
University of Miami, Miami, FL
Calvin Shedd Papers
University of Michigan, Bentley Historical Library, Ann Arbor, MI
Raymond Cazallis Davis Papers
Virginia Military Institute, Lexington, VA
Horace Meader Papers

Newspapers

Ancient City
Boston Globe
Charleston Mercury
Daytona Beach News-Journal
Florida Times Union
Newport Mercury
New Smyrna Beach Daily News
New Smyrna Beach News
New Smyrna Beach Observer
New York Herald
New York Times
Pelican
Philadelphia Inquirer
St. Augustine Evening Record

St. Augustine Examiner
St. Augustine Record
Tatler of Society in Florida

Unpublished Sources

Clark, Susan L. "Franklin W. Smith: St. Augustine's Concrete Pioneer." Master's thesis, State University of New York College at Oneonta, 1990.

Davis, James S. "Confederate Veterans Buried in St. Johns County, FL." 2008.

———. "Minorities in the Confederate Army."

Gray, Ronald N. "Edmund J. Davis: Radical Republican and Reconstruction Governor of Texas." PhD dissertation, Texas Tech University, 1976.

Greenleaf, Herbert. "History of the Confederate Monument, St. Augustine, FL."

Meyer, Marjorie G. "Venancio Sanchez: Nineteenth-Century St. Augustine Citizen." Master's thesis, Arkansas State Teachers College, 1959.

Oliver, Elizabeth Kimball. "Franklin W. Smith and His Casa Monica Hotel." Pamphlet, St. Augustine, FL: Casa Monica Hotel, 2000.

University of Florida College of Architecture. "St. Francis Inn."

———. "Study of the Tovar House." 1987.

Index

About the Author

Robert Redd is a native Floridian with a longtime interest in history. He is a graduate of Stetson University with a degree in American studies. He is a member of the St. Augustine Historical Society, the Civil War Trust and the Southeast Volusia Historical Society. This is his first book. Robert lives south of the "World's Most Famous Beach" with his wife, Christina; dogs Finley, Bessie and Jennie; and cat Ignatius.

Photo by Christina Redd.